The Phantom Letters

D1306389

Other titles of interest from Hardwood Press

Tom Pagna, with Bob Best, *Notre Dame's Era of Ara*. Foreword by Ara Parseghian.

Tom Pagna, *Letters from a Rose*. Foreword by Ara Parseghian.

THE PHANTOM SPEAKS ...

There are times when mere words smack of "corny sounds." Things sound
"corny" because they are <u>old</u>. If they are old --- there must be a part of
truth in them to have been around so long.

One word that fits the bill is <u>TRADITION</u>. To less knowledgeable people
or too young or sophisticated people, <u>TRADITION</u> is an intangible phrase.

To Notre Dame's football team, the word summarizes all that we
hold dear. It means no member of the team is greater than the team.
It means that men with common goals all aimed at one objective will rarely
bow to defeat.

Tradition means --- we will field a team of selfless people who by
doing so become bigger as individuals. It means superbly conditioned,
well prepared, and mentally tough Notre Dame Teams <u>traditionally</u> ---

1. NEVER GET INTIMIDATED !!
2. NEVER GET OUT HUSTLED OR OUT FOUGHT.
3. ALWAYS COMMAND THE RESPECT OF THE OPPONENT BECAUSE THEY REPRESENT
    THE --- CLASS OF COLLEGE FOOTBALL.

Others have paid their dues to leave you this tradition. 1973 and
all the seasons before are over. Only 1974 counts right now --- one game
at a time.

To the 1974 "Fighting Irish" The Cloak of Glorious Tradition is
awarded to you --- wearing it well is not easy, but then all things highly
prized --- never come easy.

Ga. Tech --- in the South in the heat --- the night --- the hostile
crowd can make each man feel alone. Our open secret has always been ---
"We're never alone." We're a team --- bonded together and unified. Our
strength stems from unity. As a team --- we will overcome the obstacles...

NATIONAL T.V. & GA. TECH Are early and strong tests.--- NOT IMPOSSIBLE ONES!

Let's get our first win <u>TOGETHER</u>!! GOOD LUCK & GO IRISH !!! --- MEN OF
NOTRE DAME!!!

BEAT GEORGIA TECH !!!!!!!!

The Phantom

The Phantom

Facsimile (reduced) of an original Phantom Letter (September 3, 1974).

The Phantom Letters
Motivation at Notre Dame in the Parseghian Era

Tom Pagna

Preface by Ara Parseghian

Hardwood Press
South Bend, Indiana
2005

1 2 3 4 5 6   11 10 09 08 07 06 05

Library of Congress Cataloging in Publication Data
Pagna, Tom.
The phantom letters / Tom Pagna; preface by Ara Parseghian.
p. cm.
ISBN 0-89651-558-3 (pbk.: alk. paper)
1. University of Notre Dame – Football – Correspondence.
2. Notre Dame Fighting Irish (Football team) –
Correspondence. 3. Football – Coaching – Philosophy. I. Title.
GV958.N6P34 2005
796.332'63'0977289 – dc22
2005023249

∞ The paper used in this publication meets the minimum require-
ments of the American National Standard for Information Sciences –
Permanence of Paper for Printed Materials, ANSI Z39.48-1984.

HARDWOOD PRESS
South Bend, Indiana

Contents

The Phantom Letters

The Interval That Causes Greatness

Three things comprise the "Great Interval":

    EFFORT = DO IT!

    EXECUTION = DO IT RIGHT!

    ENDURANCE = DO IT TILL IT IS DONE!

The longest play in football – a long kickoff return is approximately 12 seconds in length.

The shortest is a no-gain direct line drive. Its duration is about 2.5 seconds in length.

The average play is near to 4 seconds.

When we say INTERVAL, we are talking about that time period from the ball snap that ignites us to 4 seconds later. Nothing else really matters in a game.

On average, offense runs 80 or so plays. Defense runs nearly the same.

We are talking about 4 = 80 or 320 seconds, or about 5 minutes.

When we say INTERVAL, we are asking if you will give of EFFORT, EXECUTION AND ENDURANCE for Notre Dame – just 5 minutes worth a game. A 4-second interval by every player on every play will make us a GREAT TEAM!!

Listen and watch for the word throughout practice.

WE WILL BECOME WHAT WE DO!!!

DO THE INTERVAL!

Ara Paraseghian
(from the playbook)

The Phantom Letters of Notre Dame

In the *Era of Ara* from 1964 through the 1974 season, a written chronicle of pre-game information, slogans, mottoes, and ideals emerged.

The author was known only as the Phantom. The letters were one or two pages, written in staccato phrases, geared to thoughts that encompassed team goals and the philosophy to win. Even to this day, the identity of the PHANTOM is not certain, but ownership is not the value here; the content of the letters is. The Phantom letter prefaced *"What it will take to win,"* in the exact order of each game and each season.

Through the past 40 years, some of the Phantom letters have been lost, including some bowl games, but most of what the players saw is included in this this collection, arranged from 1966 through the Orange Bowl on January 1, 1975.

The *"Phantom Speaks"* letters were written in advance of each game and placed in each player's locker on the Monday prior to the upcoming opponent.

The phrases, sayings and emotional triggers, though sometimes repetitious, illuminate the deep philosophical targets of those Irish teams.

Simply written, with little fanfare, they are the gems of coaching thoughts. They could have been a pre-game or halftime talk. They are loaded with point-blank statements that pull no punches, telling players exactly where they are and why.

To read them is to sometimes feel you are in the locker room. Each game of each season is dated and the final outcome posted at the letters end.

Nearly one hundred letters unfold a coaching strategy, and uncommon insight into competition, and a triggering of the elements that can motivate greatness in one person or a team.

Families and businesses could profit from the uncommon, common sense. The letters are startling and open a window few have looked through.

Any fan of Notre Dame football, or any opponent who hates Notre Dame, will begin to see and understand the precarious odds such a traditional winning team faces.

Rarely has there been a more perfect view to educate the mind of the spectator, the fan, the lover of the sport of football!!

Ara Parseghian

1966

NOTRE DAME VS PURDUE
9/24/66, GAME #1

"THE PHANTOM SPEAKS"

NOTRE DAME . . . OUR TRAINING THUS FAR HAS
PUSHED SEVERAL THOUGHTS, BUT THEY ARE ONLY OF VALUE
WHEN APPLIED.

WE <u>MUST</u> BELIEVE AND PRACTICE THAT WE <u>NEVER HAVE
A BREAKING POINT!</u>

WE <u>MUST</u> PLAY WITH A FULL HEART — GIVING GREAT
EFFORT ON EACH PLAY.

IF A TEAM IS AS STRONG AS THE WEAKEST PLAYER,
EACH PLAYER MUST VOW IT IS NOT GOING TO BE
HIMSELF.

PURDUE WILL TAX US. THEY CAN RUN AND PASS. THEY
ARE DOGGED PURSUERS ON DEFENSE. THEY HAVE PRIDE,
ETC, BUT BECAUSE WE FEEL AND KNOW THROUGH PRIDE OF
BEING HERE THAT WE CAN NEVER PLAY FLAT! WE CAN
NEVER LET UP IN ANY WAY! WE MUST PLAY WITH <u>HIGH
EMOTION</u>. THE WILL TO WIN IS IN ALL PEOPLE. THOSE
WITH THE <u>MOST WILL</u> ALWAYS WIND UP WINNING! THIS IS
NATIONAL T.V. . . . THE OPENER. WE OWE PURDUE
SOMETHING SURE, BUT TO OURSELVES AND NOTRE DAME AND
THE NATION THAT FOLLOWS US WE OWE MUCH MORE.

I HAVE NO DOUBT THAT WE WILL PLAY POISED —
EMOTIONAL, WITH FIERCE PRIDE AND LOVE FOR CONTACT.
IF WE DO THESE THINGS, WE CAN START THE LONG CLIMB
TO GREATNESS!!

GOOD LUCK!!

The Phantom

FINAL
NOTRE DAME – 26   PURDUE – 14

NOTRE DAME VS NORTHWESTERN
10/1/66, GAME #2

"THE PHANTOM SPEAKS"

CONGRATULATIONS TO THE IRISH!

YOU PLAYED TO WIN AND DESERVED TO. THAT START
WAS A GOOD ONE. ONE GAME DOES NOT A SEASON MAKE!
NOT ONE PLAY OF THE PURDUE GAME WILL COUNT IN THE
WILDCAT FIASCO.

THE NORTHWESTERN GAME HAS LONG BEEN A SERIES OF
UPSETS. THEIR SEASON THUS FAR CAN BE SALVAGED — AS
ANYONE MIGHT BE IF THEY BEAT NOTRE DAME.

THE CLIMB TO THE TOP IS LIKE ONE WHO CLAWS AND
WORKS HIS WAY TO MOUNT A GREASY POLE. DARE YOU
STOP AND GLOAT HOW FAR YOU'VE COME . . . AND YOU
WILL BEGIN TO SLIP. PROGRESS MOVES ON . . . IT
CANNOT STAND STILL.

WE WILL BE AWAY, IN NORTHWESTERN'S BACKYARD.
THEY'LL SEEK REVENGE FROM LAST YEAR. YOU PLAY ONLY
AS WELL AS YOU PREPARE. PREPARE FOR A KNOCK-DOWN,
DRAG-OUT TYPE OF GAME.

BEING NOTRE DAME . . . THIS IS THE PRICE WE PAY
FOR WHATEVER FAME WE HAVE GAINED.

WE MUST HAVE DEDICATION; FULL INTERVAL — FULL
SPIRIT, AND PLAY HARD TO WIN.

THERE IS NOTHING AS IMPORTANT AS THE GAME YOU
ARE PREPARING FOR OR THE ONE YOU ARE PRESENTLY
PLAYING—

PREPARE — WORK — AND WIN.
WE ARE N O T R E   D A M E !
WE MUST PLAY LIKE IT!

The Phantom

FINAL
NOTRE DAME – 35   NORTHWESTERN – 7

NOTRE DAME VS ARMY
10/8/66, GAME #3

"THE PHANTOM SPEAKS"

THE WILDCATS ARE BEHIND US.
WE WON . . . NO ONE CAN CHANGE THAT!
AND NOW ARMY——

    THE ARMY-NOTRE DAME GAME HAS MADE <u>ALL-AMERICANS</u>
BECAUSE OF THE ATTENTION IT HAS DEMANDED. THEY ARE
UNDEFEATED, THEY WILL SEEK REVENGE. THEY HAVE
SPIRIT — TRADITION . . . AND A HISTORY OF NEVER
QUITTING. THEY ARE QUICKER THAN ANY TEAM WE HAVE
THUS FAR PLAYED.
    WE <u>CAN BE BETTER</u> THAN ARMY, BUT IT MUST BE A
CONCENTRATED EFFORT.
    <u>NO GAME IS MORE IMPORTANT THAN THE ONE YOU ARE
PREPARING FOR</u>!!!
    EACH GAME IS A "SLICE OF LIFE" TO EACH PLAYER.
IT BECOMES A PART OF A GLORIOUS HISTORY, A COLOR
PORTRAIT . . . HOW YOU PAINTED YOUR PART BECOMES
PERMANENT. THERE IS NEVER A RE-DOING OR A GOING
BACK. WHAT MUST BE DONE — <u>MUST BE DONE</u>!!
    <u>EVERY</u> EFFORT TO PROGRESS . . . WE NEED! 8 WEEKS
ARE ALL THAT ARE LEFT FOR OUR GRASP AT "GREATNESS."
WE CAN ONLY ATTACK THOSE WEEKS ONE AT A TIME!
    THIS WEEK ARMY!
    GREATNESS . . . IS NOT A MOMENT, OR A PLAY, OR
ANOTHER PLAYER. GREATNESS IS CONSISTENCY!! ALWAYS
GIVING THE SAME!!
    SOME ARE GREAT LOSERS — THEY DO IT WITH
CONSISTENCY. WE WANT TO WIN. WE ARE NOTRE DAME. IF
YOU ARE LUKE WARM ABOUT THAT - - - - YOU ARE NOT
WORTHY.
            BEAT ARMY!!!!

The Phantom

FINAL
NOTRE DAME – 35   ARMY – 0

NOTRE DAME VS NORTH CAROLINA
10/15/66, GAME #4

"THE PHANTOM SPEAKS"

CONGRATULATIONS ON YOUR ARMY WIN. 3/10 OF YOUR SEASON IS OVER. OF ALL THE GAMES THE IRISH HAVE PLAYED AND WILL PLAY. ONLY ONE IS WHAT I WORRY ABOUT AS A "SLEEPING GIANT" — NORTH CAROLINA.

YOU ARE AWARE OF OPPONENTS SUCH AS A MICHIGAN STATE, SOUTHERN CALIFORNIA, AND OKLAHOMA . . . BUT TO YOU NORTH CAROLINA APPEARS ANOTHER TEAM. B E W A R E. THEY ARE NOT — FOR THESE REASONS:

1. They are among the best-balanced group of physical specimens (225–230) with speed an agility we'll see.
2. They were off the week before they play us. They visit in full strength to see you!
3. They've beaten Michigan soundly.
4. They are seasoned, big, strong, quick.
5. They never, ever beat themselves. They are well coached and gave us a real scare last year.

WITH ALL THEIR RETURNING LETTERMAN, THEY WILL THINK ONLY OF AN UPSET.

WE CAN HAVE NO STUMBLING BLOCKS — WE CAN HAVE NO PLATEAUS — IN ORDER TO PROGRESS AS WE DID AGAINST ARMY, WE MUST "JELL" UNDER THE PRESSURE OF ONE OF THE SOUNDEST TEAMS WE WILL FACE ALL YEAR.

NO SLOGANS — NO WISDOM — JUST WORK TO GET NUMBER 4 IN OUR PATH TO BEING THE BEST. LIFE IS SHORT — WHAT WE DO WITH EVERY DAY OR EVERY GAME IS TO ALL OF US — V I T A L ! ! OPPORTUNITY KNOCKS - - - - 10 TIMES. WE'VE ANSWERED HER FIRST THREE!

THIS IS A TEAM THAT IS THE EQUAL OF PURDUE AND IN SOME PHASES, PERHAPS BETTER! WE ARE NOTRE DAME. GO . . . PROVE IT!

The Phantom

FINAL
NOTRE DAME – 32   NORTH CAROLINA – 0

6

NOTRE DAME VS OKLAHOMA
10/22/66, GAME #5

"THE PHANTOM SPEAKS"

WE HAVE COMPLETED 4/10 OF THE SEASON. EACH PART OF THE NEXT 6 PARTS WILL OFFER A DIFFERENT TYPE OF CHALLENGE. THIS WEEK IT IS THE OKLAHOMA SOONERS!
1. THEY ARE UNDEFEATED
2. THEY HAVE MOMENTUM
3. THEY HAVE THEIR HOME TOWN TO PLAY US
4. THEY ARE THE QUICKEST TEAM WE WILL PLAY
5. THEIR STRENGTH IS IN THEIR HUSTLE, SPEED, AND DESIRE.
6. THEY GANG-TACKLE AND PURSUE LIKE NO TEAM IN THE COUNTRY
7. THEY LOOK TO NOTRE DAME TO THRUST THEM INTO NATIONAL PROMINENCE.

IT IS AN OLD RIVALRY. ADMITTEDLY WE WILL NOT BE AS QUICK.

THEREFORE, WE MUST PLAY WITH A FULL HEART AND A FULL INTERVAL. THE WEATHER WILL ALSO BE TO THEIR ADVANTAGE.

WE HAVE WORKED HARD TO ACCOMPLISH WHAT WE HAVE. WE NEVER MUST ALLOW WHAT WE'VE DONE TO BE UNDONE!

IN OUR MIDST AMONG OURSELVES, WE MUST LET OUR PRIDE OVERRIDE EVERYTHING. IT MUST BE THE THING THAT DRIVES US TO IMPROVE, TO WORK, TO SACRIFICE. BEING NOTRE DAME IS NOT EASY. IF IT WERE, THEN IT WOULD NOT BE SO IMPORTANT.

EVERY MEMBER OF THE SQUAD MUST TAKE ON AND GROW LARGER EACH PRESSURING WEEK. HE MUST RECOGNIZE THAT PRESSURE PLAYERS ARE THOSE THAT IGNORE THE ROAD BEHIND AND START FROM SCRATCH.

no game is so important as
the Oklahoma Game!!!!
this week

SHUT OUT ALL OTHER INTERESTS . . . PREPARE THOROUGHLY, WITH DEDICATION, WITH ENTHUSIASM, WITH DEVOTION. SHOW IT — IT IS CATCHING. IT WILL EXPAND

US INTO AN INDIVISIBLE UNCONQUERABLE "BAND OF
IRISH," THAT NOT TEAM OR STATE . . . CAN OVERCOME.
WE ARE NOTRE DAME — ON THE FOOTBALL FIELDS —
ACROSS THE NATION — IF WE ARE, PRAY GOD TO LET US
GIVE OUR BEST TO BE WORTHY.

B E A T   O K L A H O M A ! ! !

WE CAN NEVER LET UP - - - - WE HAVE NO BREAKING
POINT!!

The Phantom

FINAL
NOTRE DAME – 38   OKLAHOMA – 0

NOTRE DAME VS NAVY
10/29/66, GAME #6

"THE PHANTOM SPEAKS"

50% OF YOUR SEASON IS OVER. YOU ARE NOW #1 IN
THE COUNTRY. THE 5 REMAINING TEAMS WILL EACH WEEK
REPRESENT AN AROUSED GROUP TO STEAL THE MARK YOU'VE
MADE.

IF WE CAN KEEP OUR HEADS, NEVER FEELING
SUPERIOR, STILL WORKING TO BE SO, IF WE CAN
DEDICATE OURSELVES TO EACH WEEK'S OPPONENT — AS
THEY COME, WE CAN BE NUMBER ONE — ALL THE WAY.
THIS WEEK — NAVY!
NAVY DOES NOT GIVE UP. THEY ARE SPIRITED, THEY
ARE BIG. FORGET WHATEVER RECORD ANY ONE MAY HAVE.
WHEN THEY PLAY THE IRISH, IT IS OF NO VALUE!
THEY'LL BE TRYING TO MAKE A <u>REPUTATION</u>. THE TOP GUN
CAN ONLY BE <u>TOP GUN</u> IF HE'S NOT TOPPED.
THIS BEING THE HALF-WAY POINT IN THE SEASON. WE
MUST CALL UPON ALL THAT MAKES WHAT WE DO IMPORTANT
— AND RE-DEDICATE — AND RE-ESTABLISH.
NO GAME IS AS IMPORTANT AS THE NAVY GAME TO US
THIS WEEK. IF YOU TAKE THEM ONE AT A TIME — THIS
MUST BE TRUE.
THEY (NAVY) WILL WORK ON THESE PREMISES.
1. N.D. — WILL RELAX VS US.
2. WE'LL BE SKY HIGH AND UPSET-MINDED.
3. THEY CAN'T KEEP THE PACE AND INJURIES ARE
   GETTING TO THEM.
4. THEY'LL BE READING THEIR PRESS CLIPPINGS AND
   IN PHILADELPHIA THE EAST LOVES NOTRE DAME.
   THEY'LL BASK IN GLORY AND NOT BE QUITE SO
   "READY."
5. WE'VE NOTHING TO LOSE AND WE'LL SHOOT THE
   WORKS.
NOTRE DAME MUST WORK ON THESE PREMISES!!
OUR LIVES ARE WRAPPED UP IN NOTRE DAME — IN
FOOTBALL — IN THE 1966 SEASON. WE WANT IT TO BE
THE BEST EVER. NO RIPENESS, NO LACK OF EFFORT, NO
FALSE ESTEEM FROM BEING NUMBER ONE IS GOING TO

9

CHEAT US OUT OF BEING READY. WE HAVE MADE THE
STRETCH TURN TOWARDS GREAT PROMISE. WE ARE NOTRE
DAME — APART, DIFFERENT . . . BECAUSE WE WORK AT
IT!!!

    LET NO NOTRE DAME MAN ——— LET UP.

    LET NO NOTRE DAME MAN ——— VARY FROM THE COURSE
WE'VE SET.

    INDIVIDUALLY WE ARE CAPABLE OF BEING — COMMON —
VERY COMMON. BUT COUPLED WITH TEAM BONDS, WITH
COMMON ENTHUSIASM WITH UNDYING UNITY, AND LOYALTY —
NO ONE CAN OVERCOME US.

      COME ON NAVY — TAKE YOUR POT SHOT —
      THEY ALL WANT TO!!

The Phantom

FINAL
NOTRE DAME – 31   NAVY – 7

NOTRE DAME VS PITTSBURGH
11/5/66, GAME #7

"THE PHANTOM SPEAKS"

WE NOW FACE PITTSBURGH — THE CLASSICAL, THE
HAVES AGAINST THE HAVE-NOTS!

I WONDER IF THEY KNOW THE <u>HAVES</u> ARE PHYSICALLY
HURTING, OR THAT THEY FEEL THE DRAG OF A LONG
SEASON. I WONDER IF "REVENGE" WORKS FOR OPPONENTS
. . . AS THEY THINK OF LAST YEAR'S 69-13 STOMPING.

I WONDER IF THE IRISH CAN STAND UP TO THE IDEAL
OF PLAYING GAMES ONE AT A TIME. NO GAME AS
IMPORTANT AS THE ONE YOU'RE PLAYING!

WE WERE NOT SHARP AGAINST NAVY. THE DEFENSE
PLAYED SPLENDIDLY!

BUT OUR OFFENSE LACKED EXPLOSIVENESS!

WHY CAN'T THE REGNERS, GOEDDEKES, CONJARS,
SEILERS —— RECOGNIZE THAT 4 WEEKS MORE CAN
IMMORTALIZE THEIR PLAYING CAREERS, THAT WE HAVE A
CHANCE THAT FEW OTHERS WILL EVER REALIZE IN THEIR
LIFETIMES. <u>IF WE CAN GRASP THIS — IF WE CHOOSE TO
GIVE OUR BEST — FOUR WEEKS MORE — ONE WEEK AT A
TIME</u>, <u>NOTRE DAME AND HER MEN AND THEIR FUTURES WILL
LIGHT UP WITH LUSTER</u>. <u>INTENSIFY</u> — EVERYTHING YOU
DO.

WORK!!! BE THE GUY WHO SPARKS THE REST. IF YOU
ARE A <u>SENIOR —</u>, KNOW THAT "YOU WILL NEVER PASS
THIS WAY AGAIN."

<u>PLAY YOUR HEARTS OUT</u>, <u>WHENEVER YOU PLAY FOR
NOTRE DAME</u>.

B E A T   P I T T S B U R G H
(FINALLY, TOTALLY, AND EXCLUSIVELY)
(NOTHING OF CONCERN BEYOND THAT!)

THIS IS THE NEXT TO LAST TIME YOU'LL PLAY AT
AND IN NOTRE DAME'S STADIUM ————— MAKE IT
MEMORABLE!

The Phantom

FINAL
NOTRE DAME – 40   PITTSBURGH – 0

NOTRE DAME VS DUKE
11/5/66, GAME #8

"THE PHANTOM SPEAKS"

THIS GAME WITH DUKE IS THE LAST TIME SENIORS WILL PLAY BEFORE A NOTRE DAME CROWD IN THEIR HOME STADIUM!

WE MUST RESPECT DUKE! PITTSBURGH SHOULD HAVE TAUGHT US THAT! WE CAN LOOK AHEAD AND PLAY WITH NO FIERCENESS AGAIN. BUT IS THAT THE LAST MEMORY YOU WANT TO HOLD?

SENIORS	SENIORS
LYNCH	CONJAR
PAGE	EDDY
DURANKO	REGNER
RHOADS	SEILER
HORNEY	GOEDDEKE
HARDY	SWATLAND

SENIORS: NO GAME IS AS IMPORTANT AS YOUR GAME WITH DUKE — YOUR LAST APPEARANCE FOR NOTRE DAME ON YOUR HOME FIELD!

The Phantom

FINAL
NOTRE DAME – 64   DUKE – 0

NOTRE DAME VS MICHIGAN STATE
11/19/66, GAME #9

"THE PHANTOM SPEAKS"

ONE YEAR AGO MICHIGAN STATE BEAT US.

I REMEMBER THEIR DEFENSE SCREAMING AT US FROM
THE SIDELINES — THEY LOOKED LIKE KAMIKAZES'
"CRAZED" MADNESS. THEY SWORE AT US — THEY TOOK US
OUT OF BOUNDS — THEY FOREARMED ILLEGALLY TO THE
FACE, THEY HIT AND SWARMED AND PILED AFTER THE
WHISTLE. WHEN WE LOOKED AT FILM, WE WERE AMAZED
THAT SO FEW STATE PLAYERS WERE KNOCKED OFF THEIR
FEET. WE WERE "OUT-BLUFFED!" THEY SHOWED
AGGRESSIVENESS — YELLING AND SCREAMING — ONE THING
BURNED MY EARS AND STUCK WITH ME — THEIR LINEBACKER
THORNHILL SAID, "YOU DON'T WANT IT!"
MAYBE THEY BLUFFED US INTO THINKING NO ONE COULD
PASS OR RUN. THEY BULLIED US INTO BEING AWED OF
THEIR ABILITY. ONE THING I DO KNOW — THIS YEAR WE
WANT IT! I KNOW THEY'LL TRY ALL THE SAME TACTICS.
I KNEW A BULLY ONCE IN SCHOOL WHO BACKED ME DOWN
BY WORDS AND TOUGH GESTURES UNTIL I HATED TO DO
THAT. I GOT THE FIRST PUNCH AT HIM AND NEVER ONCE
QUIT——— AND I BACKED HIM DOWN!!
TOGETHER WE HAVE TO STAND SO UNITED, SO STRONG,
SO FEROCIOUS, THAT WE'LL NOT ONLY BLOCK AND TACKLE
THEM — WE'LL WAGE PERSONAL WARS. THE WORST THING
YOU CAN DO TO THEM IS BEAT THEM.
THEY ARE NOT SUPERMEN, THEY SWARM YOU AND TRY TO
GET BELLIGERENT ENOUGH TO FORCE YOU TO BACK OFF.
THOUGH I WON'T SAY WE BACKED OFF LAST YEAR — WE
WERE NOT PREPARED FOR THE ASSAULT, THE BULLYING.
THIS YEAR WILL BE DIFFERENT. WE'RE GOING AFTER
THEM! WE WANT IT — THORNHILL, WEBSTER, SMITH,
JONES, WASHINGTON — WHEN YOU HIT THEM — AND THEY
FALL — YOU'LL BEGIN TO KNOW — THEY ARE VULNERABLE.
WE NEED GREAT TEAM PRIDE!
WE NEED GREAT TEAM SPIRIT!
WE NEED GREAT EFFORT AND HUSTLE!
WE NEED THE ELEMENT THAT MAKES NOTRE DAME GREAT!

THE FIRE OF A FULL HEART!

THE WILL TO WIN — THE INCOMPARABLE SPIRIT OF NO BREAKING POINT. THE PRIDE INDIVIDUALLY THAT SAYS — "I WILL PLAY MY GREATEST GAME, GIVE MY GREATEST EFFORT," CANNOT BE DENIED.

WE MUST NOT BE DENIED!!
WE WON'T BE DENIED!!

The Phantom

FINAL
NOTRE DAME – 10   MICHIGAN STATE – 10

NOTRE DAME VS SOUTHERN CAL
11/19/66, GAME #10

"THE PHANTOM SPEAKS"

IRISH! YOU ARE HURTING . . . BUT UNBOWED AND
UNBEATEN. THERE ARE NO SOPHOMORES ON OUR SQUAD.
HAVING LIVED AND FOUGHT YOUR WAY BACK AGAINST
MICHIGAN STATE MADE ALL OF YOU GROW UP . . .
BEYOND ANY POINT OF INEXPERIENCE.

SOUTHERN CAL OUT THERE IS DIFFERENT FROM ANY
WERE ELSE IN THE WORLD.

I REMEMBER THE "IRISH" SQUAD WALKING THE LONG
EMPTY WALK FROM THE FIELD TO THE TUNNEL. I REMEMBER
THEIR FULL-GROWN BODIES — SHAKING WITH SOBS OF
DEJECTION. I RECALL THE FANTASTIC TURN OF EVENTS
THAT ROBBED US OF A NATIONAL CHAMPIONSHIP.

WE NEVER CRIED FOUL!

WE'RE GOING BACK THERE. THE ODDS ARE THESE: THEY
ARE A GOOD SOUND, QUICK FOOTBALL TEAM ON THEIR HOME
FIELD. WE MUST TRAVEL THERE AND PLAY IN WARM
WEATHER AND OVERCOME THEIR HOME ADVANTAGES. WE MUST
BLOT OUT ANY OUTSIDE THOUGHT — BECAUSE THEY ALWAYS
ATTEMPT TO SWARM OUR VISIT THERE WITH KINDNESS. THE
RELAXING "HAPPY CARNIVAL ATMOSPHERE" THAT LULLS YOU
INTO EASY PREY.

WE ARE FIGHTERS — HURT THOUGHT WE MAY BE! — WE
ARE AWARE OF ALL THE OBSTACLES, ALL THE MEMORIES.

A LAST GOODBYE — A LAST-DITCH EFFORT — A LAST
GESTURE FOR OUR LADY OF NOTRE DAME CAN OVERCOME
ALL.

    G O   I R I S H —— BECOME UNDEFEATED!!!!
         THE CHAMPIONS YOU ARE!!

The Phantom

FINAL
NOTRE DAME – 51   SOUTHERN CAL – 0

1967

THE PHANTOM SPEAKS EARLY
PRE-SEASON LETTER
1967

IRISH OF 1967
"ALL YOU HAVE IS A REPUTATION . . ."
YOU CLAIM PRIDE — TRADITION — SPIRIT —— BUT
THESE ARE EMPTY CLAIMS OF A NEW UNTESTED GROUP.

THE 1966 TEAM WON THE HONOR . . . YOU INHERITED
IT. IT WAS A LEGACY, A GIFT AND A FLEETING ONE —
UNLESS:

YOU LEARN TEAM UNITY! YOU GATHER PRIDE AND
ONENESS!

YOUR PRACTICES REFLECT ENTHUSIASM. NO ONE REALLY
LEADS AS A PLAYER . . .

HE LEADS A LITTLE OF HIMSELF. . . IT BECOMES
CONTAGIOUS.

LOAF JUST A LITTLE, NOW MULTIPLY A LITTLE TIMES
THE NUMBER ON THE TEAM.

START THE CLIMB TOWARD—— THE REALITY OF THE
REPUTATION TO MAKE IT MEAN SOMETHING — NOT FOR 1966
— THEY'RE GONE—— BUT TO 1967 — HERE AND NOW!

The Phantom

NOTRE DAME VS CALIFORNIA
9/23/67, GAME #1

"THE PHANTOM SPEAKS DEEPLY"

THERE IS A SHALLOW RING TO MOST WORDS. USUALLY
BECAUSE THEY HAVE BEEN OVER USED, MISUSED, OR NEVER
USED.

BUT MOST ALWAYS, THE EMPTY MEANINGLESS <u>BLAH</u> IS
CAUSED FROM APATHY — THE UTTER INDIFFERENCE OF A
MEDIOCRE PERSON.

WHERE TEAMS ARE CONCERNED, NO ONE MUST FEEL BLAH
— OR MEDIOCRE. THE ADRENALIN MUST FLOW WITHOUT
BEING FORCED FROM THE OUTSIDE OR . . . MERE
SURFACE MOTIVES. THE INNER ANXIETY THAT EACH PLAYER
BUILDS IS TRUE "CONCERN." TRUE CONCERN BUILDS TEAM
PRIDE . . . IT BONDS TOGETHER . . . IT BLOTS OUT
THE UNWANTED DISTRACTION.

BACK TO WORDS — WE HAVE COINED PHRASES . . . WE
HAVE BELIEVED IN THEM. WE HAVE PROVEN THEM TRUE .
. . THESE CANNOT WEAR THIN . . . THEY MUST REMAIN
TRUE.
1. NO GAME IS AS IMPORTANT AS THE GAME WE ARE
   GOING TO PLAY SEPT. 23.
2. NOTRE DAME CAN HAVE NO BREAKING POINT.
3. WE WILL BECOME WHAT WE DO . . . THEREFORE, TO
   BE W I N N E R S. WE MUST WIN!
4. TO WIN . . . WE MUST PAY THE PRICE!

THIS 4-POINTED LOGIC MUST CAPTURE EACH MAN'S
MIND. UNTIL OUR
TEAM HAS BONDED ITSELF AGAINST ALL OPPONENTS.

NOTRE DAME HAS A GREAT PAST — HER HISTORY IS
NOW BEING ADDED ON TO BY OUR — 1967 TEAM.

GO IRISH!

The Phantom

FINAL
NOTRE DAME – 41   CALIFORNIA – 8

NOTRE DAME VS PURDUE
9/30/67, GAME #2

"THE PHANTOM SPEAKS"

YOUR 1967 RECORD IS ONE WIN. JUST ONE!

THE FIRST BIG COLLEGE FOOTBALL WEEKEND IS OVER. MANY SCHOOLS PICKED TO WIN — <u>DID NOT</u>! OUR BREAKING POINT <u>WAS NOT TAXED!</u>

PURDUE . . . REPRESENTS A RUGGED TOUGH AND TALENTED OPPONENT. THEY ALSO GAIN THE ADVANTAGE OF PLAYING US IN THEIR HOME STADIUM. OUR LAST VISIT THERE WAS IN 1965, WHEN WE CAME HOME ON THE SHORT END OF THE SCORE.

NOTHING SHORT OF AN ALL-OUT TEAM EFFORT — SUPERB DEFENSE AND AN INSPIRED OFFENSE WILL — ALLOW US VICTORY.

WE MUST EXECUTE OUR GAME PLAN WITH ALL THE FIRE AND WILL A NOTRE DAME TEAM CAN MUSTER.

IN ONLY THE SECOND WEEK OF OUR SCHEDULE . . . WE ARE MEETING ONE OF OUR TOUGHEST OPPONENTS. THE PURDUE GAME IS TRADITIONALLY A KNOCK-DOWN, DRAG-OUT WAR. THEY WILL COME AFTER US WITH EVERYTHING THEY OWN. OUR STRENGTHS MUST BE IN OUR TEAM UNITY AND DEDICATION TO PURPOSE. THE PURPOSE IS TO WIN . . . OVER PURDUE . . . NO MISTAKES . . . NO PENALTIES . . . NO FUMBLES . . . AND NO EFFORT LESS THAN YOUR BEST!

POISE UNDER FIRE IS THE EARMARK OF A GREAT COMPETITOR. WE WILL ALL HAVE A CHANCE TO PROVE OUR MEASURE OF GREATNESS . . . THERE WILL BE <u>FIRE</u>!

NO GAME IS AS IMPORTANT TO NOTRE DAME AS . . . THE <u>P U R D U E</u> GAME ON SEPTEMBER 30, 1967.

BEAT THE — BOILERMAKERS!

The Phantom

FINAL
NOTRE DAME – 21   PURDUE – 28

NOTRE DAME VS IOWA
10/7/67, GAME #3

"THE PHANTOM SPEAKS"

"IF YOU CAN MEET WITH TRIUMPH & DISASTER, AND
TREAT THOSE TWO IMPOSTORS JUST THE SAME!"
WE ARE NEVER ALLOWED TO ENJOY A VICTORY FOR MORE
THAN A DAY . . . NOR SHOULD WE DOTE ON A LOSS ANY
LONGER. IT IS OVER . . . WE ALL HATE TO LOSE . . .
WE NEVER WANT TO BE GOOD LOSERS . . . IT IS A
ROTTEN — FATIGUING EMPTY DISILLUSIONMENT. WINNING
IS THE ONLY REWARD.
WE HAVE KNOWN SUCCESS . . . IT DIDN'T MAKE US
FAT, DID IT? DID IT WARP OUR REASON INTO THINKING
WE COULD CONQUER ALL WITH JUST TOKEN EFFORTS? IOWA
IS OUR NEXT CHALLENGE — THERE IS NO GAME SO
IMPORTANT AS THE IOWA GAME. SOMEWHERE WE MUST
REMOLD AN IRON-CLAD UNITY, AN ARMOR OF "PRIDE" THAT
EACH MEMBER OF THE IRISH SQUAD CONTRIBUTES TO WITH
A FULL HEART. THE WEAK FALL AWAY — BUT THOSE WITH
"WINNING BLOOD" REBOUND — THEY BOUNCE BACK FROM
EVERY BLOW THAT LIFE CAN DEAL — WITH A ZEST, A
HEROIC OPTIMISM — A FIERY SPIRIT THAT PERPETUALLY
REDEDICATES.
NOTRE DAME . . . "OUR MOTHER" IS THE SYMBOL
THAT EMBODIES OUR PRIDE . . . OUR VERY SPIRIT THAT
IN THE PAST HAS CAUSED US SUCH "FAMILY PRIDE AND
DEDICATION." IT WAS ALWAYS SO GENUINE — WE NEVER
PLAYED A FLAT GAME. OUR SPIRIT WAS NEVER PHONY —
NEVER FORCED. SUCCESS ONLY WHETTED APPETITES. DID
WE TAKE SUCCESS FOR GRANTED? DID OUR NOTRE DAME
HUNGER SUBSIDE INTO MEDIOCRE EMOTION? . . . THE
GREAT EFFORT IS A PRICE EACH PLAYER OWES. BUT ONLY
IF NOTRE DAME IS TO REMAIN — SOMETHING SPECIAL,
SOMETHING WONDERFULLY DIFFERENT, THE UNIQUE —
HUNGRY — EFFORT OF TRUE PRIDE.

REBOUND . . . DON'T BE GUILTY OF TOO LITTLE
EFFORT, EXECUTION ENDURANCE!

BEAT IOWA!

The Phantom

FINAL
NOTRE DAME – 56   IOWA – 6

NOTRE DAME VS SOUTHERN CALIFORNIA
10/14/67, GAME #4

"THE PHANTOM SPEAKS"

SOUTHERN CALIFORNIA TRIES TO MAN ON MAN BLOCK —
SWARM ON DEFENSE AND EMPLOY THEIR GREAT TEAM SPEED,
TO OVERWHELM OPPONENTS. THEY REPRESENT THE TOP TEAM
IN THE COUNTRY . . . COMING HERE TO SEEK REVENGE
FOR 1966. WE CAN BEAT THEM. THERE IS NO FORTRESS
OF PLAYERS THAT CAN WITHSTAND THE ONSLAUGHT OF PURE
DESIRE. DESIRE THAT CREEPS INTO PLAYERS
INDIVIDUALLY AND SLOWLY CLIMBS TO A PEAK OF GREAT
TEAM DESIRE — KNOWS NO BOUNDS!

WE MUST WANT TO WIN SO BADLY THAT EVERY EFFORT
AND EVERY MOVEMENT IS AN UNHARNESSED ATTEMPT TO
PERSONALLY MAKE THE PLAY!

OUR DEFENSE MUST PREPARE FOR THEIR GREATEST
CHALLENGE. O.J. IS OUR JOB.

ON OFFENSE — WE MUST POSSESS THE BALL WITH
MACHINE-LIKE EXECUTION AND SCORE!

WHATEVER EXTRA EACH PLAYER SUMMONS FOR HIMSELF
TO BE THIS WEEK, MULTIPLY BY 22. LET US SAY THAT
EACH PLAYER CONTRIBUTES AN OUNCE OF EFFORT OVER HIS
NORM. HE ALSO CONTRIBUTES A "PINCH" OF DESIRE, A
HEART FULL OF PRIDE & EFFORT! THESE NARROW MARGINS
— MULTIPLIED BY THE 22 PLAYERS ON OFFENSE & DEFENSE
CAN BE THE FACTOR. TALK IS CHEAP! DON'T THINK IT —
DO IT!

BEAT SOUTHERN CALIFORNIA!

GREAT ACHIEVEMENT IS NEVER THE PRODUCT OF
SENTIMENT — IT IS THE INSPIRED CRAVING OF THOSE WHO
THIRST & HUNGER FOR SUCCESS.

MENTALLY-FAT PEOPLE — LOSE THIS!

The Phantom

FINAL
NOTRE DAME – 7   SOUTHERN CAL – 24

NOTRE DAME VS ILLINOIS
10/21/67, GAME #5

"THE PHANTOM SPEAKS"

IN THE PAST YEARS OF NOTRE DAME FOOTBALL —
VICTORY WAS NEVER ACHIEVED BECAUSE OF SUPER-HUMAN
PLAYERS . . . AND NO ONE EXPECTS YOU TO BE. NOTRE
DAME PLAYERS WERE DIFFERENT THOUGH . . . GIVING
SUPER HUMAN EFFORT. THAT EFFORT WAS ALWAYS THE
ELEMENT THAT OPPONENTS COULD NOT MATCH. THIS EFFORT
WAS NOT LACKING VS SOUTHERN CALIFORNIA, BUT FOR ALL
THE EFFORT . . . <u>MISTAKES</u> NEUTRALIZED THE EFFECT.
AND NOW THE REAL TEST . . . "IF YOU CAN WATCH
THE THINGS YOU GAVE YOUR LIFE TO, BROKEN — AND
STOOP TO BUILD THEM UP WITH WORN OUT TOOLS."

OR

"IF YOU CAN FORCE YOUR HEART & NERVE & SINEW TO
SERVE THEIR TURN . . . LONG AFTER THEY ARE GONE."

OR

BOUNCING UP . . . RECOILING BACK & NOT — JUST
CRUMPLING — REQUIRES A BEAUTIFUL ENTHUSIASM. ONLY
GREAT HEARTS POSSESS OPTIMISM & ENTHUSIASM IN THE
WAKE OF PAST DEFEATS.
LESSER MEN . . . . LESSER HEARTS . . . . YIELD!
A TRUE WINNER . . . A NOTRE DAME MAN LOSES
POORLY — SO POORLY HE FIGHTS BACK & CLAWS & CLIMBS
& BOUNCES . . . SO THAT HE MAY BE DOWN BUT NEVER
EVER COUNTED OUT.
"WE ARE THIS BREED" THE COACHES, THE PLAYERS,
THE SCHOOL.

       AND YOUR EFFORT
       AND YOUR ENTHUSIASM
       WORK TO CORRECT MISTAKES

TRUE WORTH IS NEVER KNOWN IF IT KNOWS NO TEST.
TEST TIME FOR 6 MORE WEEKS — AND ILLINOIS — THERE
IS THE START!

THE PHANTOM & THE GHOSTS OF NOTRE DAME CHALLENGE YOU TO RESPOND.

The Phantom

FINAL
NOTRE DAME – 47   ILLINOIS – 7

NOTRE DAME VS MICHIGAN STATE
10/28/67, GAME #6

"THE PHANTOM SPEAKS"

THERE WAS MORE "IRISH TRADITION," MORE "NOTRE
DAME TEAM SPIRIT," MORE UNIFICATION OF EFFORT
TOWARD A GOAL VS THE ILLINI. WE DIDN'T LOOK GREAT
. . . BUT IMPROVED . . . & MOST IMPORTANT . . . WE
WON!

MICHIGAN STATE IS COMING HERE TO PLAY A LONG-
AWAITED GRUDGE MATCH. TO BE SURE THEY WILL BE FIRED
TO THE HILT. MORE THAN ANY TIME THIS SEASON, WE
MUST DRAW OURSELVES TOGETHER IN A BOND OF
TEAMSMANSHIP — NO OUTSIDE FORCE & ESPECIALLY
SPARTAN FORCE CAN BE ALLOWED TO SHAKE US.

THEY WILL SCREAM AT YOU — HOLD YOU — INTIMIDATE
YOU — TRY TO PSYCH OR BLUFF YOU INTO RELENTING.
THIS IS THEIR WAY, BUT WE ARE READY TO COME OF AGE
. . . THE AGE OF "MENTAL TOUGHNESS" — THE ATTITUDE
OF GREAT HUSTLING. D E S I R E, AND RAW, NAKED
P R I D E — THE FRAME OF MIND THAT SAYS — NOTHING
IS MORE IMPORTANT THAN THIS GAME!!

IRISH — HAVE YOU EVER BEEN IN A SITUATION WHERE
PRIDE AND ALL PRESS YOU INTO AN OPEN FIGHT? THIS
SATURDAY WILL BE SUCH A GAME. CERTAINLY MEN FEEL
APPREHENSION — THEY WORRY — THEY SHOW CONCERN — BUT
THE GREAT BATTLERS, THE COMPETITORS WITH FULL
HEARTS, OVERCOME ALL OF IT WHEN THE BELL RINGS.

WE MUST NOT MAKE MISTAKES!

WE MUST NOT HAVE TURNOVERS, MISSED TACKLES, OR
MISSED ASSIGNMENTS!

WE MUST PLAY THE GAME NOT OVER TIGHT — YET
SUFFICIENTLY KEYED TO GIVE OUR FINEST EFFORT.

THE WORLD TURNS — & TURNS AWAY FROM LOSERS —
WINNERS ARE ALL THAT ARE RECOGNIZED . . . AND
RIGHTLY SO, AS WINNERS ARE A BREED THAT TAP A
GREAT RESERVOIR OF ABILITY . . . CALLED SIMPLY, IT
IS D E S I R E! A GREAT PART OF TALENT IS WANTING
TO . . . THE DESIRE TO WIN SHOULD PERMEATE OUR
EVERY MOMENT OF PREPARATION. WORK! SWEAT! AND GET
MENTALLY TOUGH FOR THIS CONTEST.

EACH MAN ON THE FIELD IS MARKED BY THE TRADITION
THAT IS NOTRE DAME . . . HE IS BEYOND BEING MARKED
— EXPECTED — HE FURTHER EXPECTS — TO GIVE HIS BEST
& WHIP ONE MAN ON EACH PLAY.
                    JUST ONE MAN!
IF 10 DO IT — AND YOU WHO READ THIS DON'T, IT IS
NOT ENOUGH!!! IF ELEVEN DO . . . . ! WE   CAN
OVERCOME   THE   SPARTANS.

    TALK IS CHEAP, ACTION'IS FORTUNE. YOUR YEARS AT
NOTRE DAME PASS QUICKLY — YOU WILL NEVER PASS THIS
WAY AGAIN!!!

        B E A T   M S U !!!

The Phantom

FINAL
NOTRE DAME – 24   MICHIGAN STATE – 12

NOTRE DAME VS NAVY
11/4/67, GAME #7

"THE PHANTOM SPEAKS"

FOR ONE HALF, WE LOOKED LIKE THE IRISH OF OLD.
WE WERE HUNGRY BLOCKING AND TACKLING AGGRESSIVELY.
WE HAD PURPOSE. WE THEN SMEARED THE GLOSS OF A
REAL GOOD WIN BY SLOWING OUR TEMPO. WE MISSED
TACKLES, AND DIDN'T SWARM. WE FUMBLED THE BALL.
EVERY FUMBLE IS WORTH 40 YARDS. 5 OF THEM, 2 ON
EXCHANGES, BLEIER, HANRATTY, AND ZIMMERMAN. THIS
KILLS A GOOD TEAM. WITH ALL OF THAT, WE WON, BUT
THE SWEET TASTE OF VICTORY DAMNED NEAR TURNED SOUR.

AS YET WE HAVEN'T PUT THE THING TOGETHER. TOUGH
DEFENSE AND CONSISTENT ERRORLESS OFFENSE . . . FOR
60 COMPLETE MINUTES. WE ARE PAST THE HALF-WAY MARK,
SO THERE ARE NO SOPHOMORES. WE ALL KNOW WHAT IT IS
ABOUT NOW.

NAVY — QUICK, ALERT, 4 & 2 RECORD, GREAT
CONDITIONING, GREAT MORALE — WILL TRY TO MAKE ITS
SEASON AT YOUR EXPENSE. THEY WON'T FOLD — THEY
WON'T QUIT — THEY PROBABLY WERE LOOKING FORWARD TO
YOU WHEN THEY SQUEAKED BY PITT.

LOGIC TELLS THE WORLD . . . & SO YOU CAN'T SAY
YOU HAVEN'T BEEN TOLD . . . THERE WILL BE A
TENDENCY FOR RELAXING AFTER BEATING MSU
            WE CAN'T AFFORD THE LUXURY!

RECOGNIZE WHAT A GREAT THRILL IT WAS WHEN WE
WERE READY TO FIRST TAKE THE FIELD AGAINST THE
SPARTANS. WE WERE PREPARED TO DO BATTLE — CHARGED
WITH ELECTRICITY, FILLED WITH BUT ONE UNIFIED IDEA
— TO W I N !

OUR IDEA IS TO GO ALL THE WAY — IMPROVING ON
THE WAY. WE CAN'T RELAX — OR LET UP . . . N A V Y
IS   S O U N D. IT IS OF NO VALUE TO WIN A BIG ONE
AND FALL AFTERWARDS—— THERE IS NO GAME OF MORE
IMPORTANCE RIGHT NOW, THAN NAVY.

PEOPLE HAVE WRITTEN "KOOK" LETTERS WHO HAVE SEEN
YOU PLAY — "THEY SAY WE LET UP," "WERE SLOPPY,"
"WE HAVE NO KILLER INSTINCT" . . .

MEN OF NOTRE DAME, APPEAL TO YOURSELVES FOR FOUR

29

MORE WEEKS — FOR FOUR 60 MINUTE GAMES . . . GIVE -
110% OF YOUR EFFORT. ANY ONE CAN BE MEDIOCRE . . .
NOTRE DAME DESERVES MORE!
B E A T   N A V Y !

The Phantom

FINAL
NOTRE DAME – 43   NAVY – 15

NOTRE DAME VS PITTSBURGH
11/11/67, GAME #8

"THE PHANTOM SPEAKS"

IRISH . . . THE POOREST GAME LAST YEAR'S TEAM PLAYED WAS AGAINST PITT. THEY THOUGHT IT WOULD BE A CAKE WALK — AND AT THE HALF OUR STUMBLING AND FUMBLING AROUND SAW ONLY A 7-TO-0 LEAD.

THEIR PLAYERS WANT TO WIN AS BADLY AS WE DO . . . THEY ARE OF EQUAL SIZE . . . THEY HAVE NOTHING TO LOSE . . . THEY WILL GIVE A KAMIKAZE EFFORT . . . AN UPSET OVER US IS THE LEAST CONSIDERED THOUGHT — SO THEY HOPE WE CAN BELIEVE THAT.

OUR PROBLEM IS SIMPLY THIS — WE CAN BE A GOOD SOUND FOOTBALL TEAM — GO AFTER THEM — BEAT THEM AND FORGET IT. THE REASON THAT THIS IS DIFFICULT LIES IN THE "STATE OF MIND" IN WHICH YOU APPROACH THAT GAME. "A N Y" T E A M C A N B E K N O C K E D O F F.

GREAT COMPETITORS COME TO PLAY . . . PLAY THEIR BEST — WITH FULL HEARTS! LET'S JUST GO AFTER THEM THAT WAY — IT IS ONE MORE STEP, WE NEED TO APPROACH THE END OF THE SEASON WITH CLEAN SLATES.

H A V E   T R U E   P R I D E ! !
B E A T   P I T T S B U R G H !

The Phantom

FINAL
NOTRE DAME – 38   PITTSBURGH – 0

NOTRE DAME VS GEORGIA TECH
11/18/67, GAME #9

"THE PHANTOM SPEAKS"

WE ARE 8/10 OF THE SEASON FINISHED. THE NEXT TWO
AND MORE SPECIFICALLY GEORGIA TECH AND MIAMI
REPRESENT A WORLD OF DIFFERENCE FOR US.
THEY ARE SOUTHERN TEAMS, THEY POINT ALL YEAR
LONG TO PLAYING THE IRISH. THEY HAVE THEIR CLIMATE,
THEIR HOME FIELD AND HOME CROWD.
WHEN THE SEASON STARTS TO END, IT IS EASY TO
RELAX — TO LET UP — TO GO THROUGH THE MOTIONS. WE
CAN BE NO WORSE THAN 6 & 4 . . . IF WE JUST LAY
DOWN! WE COULD ALSO BE 8 & 2 . . . IF WE WOULD
ENJOY BEING IN THE TOP TEN . . . AND FIND ENOUGH
MORALE, SPIRIT, LOVE OF NOTRE DAME TO PRESS ON
. . . WHEN PRESSING ON GETS TOUGH! WE HAVE RUN A
GOOD RACE TILL HERE . . . WILL WE FINISH? CAN WE
FORCE "OUR HEART & NERVE & SINEW TO SERVE THEIR
TURN, LONG AFTER THEY ARE GONE?"
CAN WE OVERCOME ALL THE DISTRACTIONS OF PLAYING
AWAY — OUT OF OUR CLIMATE . . . AND HOLD TRUE TO
OUR OWN CREED . . . FULL HEART — NO BREAKING POINT
— FULL INTERVAL? IF WE DO LESS, WE GAVE SO MUCH
FOR SO LITTLE. ALL THE WAY IS OUR CRY! GO GET THE
GEORGIA TECH TEAM 1ST! LET'S "GUT UP" FOR TWO MORE
WEEKS — TWO MORE EFFORTS — TWO MORE WINS.
NO GAME IS SO IMPORTANT THAN GEORGIA TECH
. . . THIS WEEK.
G R E A T N E S S IS PRESSING ON WHEN PRESSING
ON IS THE TOUGHEST THING LEFT TO DO . . . THAT IS
WHY THERE ARE FEW TRULY GREAT TEAMS. WE CAN BE!!

The Phantom

FINAL
NOTRE DAME – 36   GEORGIA TECH – 3

NOTRE DAME VS MIAMI (FLA)
11/24/67, GAME #10

"THE PHANTOM SPEAKS"

THOSE OF YOU WHO PLAYED AT MIAMI IN 1965 — TELL THOSE ON THE SQUAD WHO DIDN'T!

TELL THEM HOW CRAZY MAD THE CROWD WAS — THE NOISE, THE BAND BEATING DRUMS WHEN WE ARE ON OFFENSE. TELL THEM THAT WE ARE FORCED TO WEAR DARK COLORS UNDER THE LIGHTS BECAUSE MIAMI <u>INSISTS</u> ON WEARING WHITE. TELL THEM THAT MIAMI PURPOSELY SCHEDULES THE "IRISH" WITH A WEEK OFF BEFORE.

THEY WILL BE FIRED TO THE HILT, "LYING IN THE WEEDS FOR US." THEY TIED US 0-0 WITH THE AID OF AN OFFICIAL'S CALL IN 1965. IT WAS THEIR MORAL VICTORY."

THEY ARE TOUGH, BIG, FAST — IT WILL TAKE OUR VERY BEST EFFORT TO BEAT THEM. DARE YOU NOT WIN — THEY WILL THROW THINGS, SWEAR AND DEGRADE. ALL THESE PEOPLE REALLY BOW TO IS THE WINNER. JUST AS IN GEORGIA TECH'S STADIUM WHEN IT WAS OVER, THEY <u>KNEW</u> WHY PEOPLE RESPECTED NOTRE DAME!

WHY MUST WE TAKE THIS GAME SO REALLY "B I G"?

1. IT IS THE LAST TIME SCHOEN, O'LEARY, SMITHBERGER, MCGILL, PERGINE, MARTIN, HARDY, HARSHMAN, QUINN, SWATLAND, . . . & BLEIER WILL WEAR NOTRE DAME'S GOLD AND BLUE. BLEIER MAY NOT BE ABLE TO PLAY OR EVEN ATTEND . . . WINNING ONE FOR THE "ROCK" TAKES A NEWER MEANING.
2. WE OWE MIAMI SOMETHING!
3. WE CAN FINISH WAY UP IN THE TOP 10 & SALVAGE A GREAT FIGHT-BACK SEASON — SHOWING EVERYONE & OURSELVES, WE HAD THE MOXIE NEVER TO QUIT REGARDLESS OF CIRCUMSTANCES.
4. <u>THIS IS OUR BOWL GAME</u>.

NO 4-DAY VACATION CAN BE FUN, IF WE CANNOT ENJOY VICTORY. LET'S SELL OUT — GREAT HITTING (THEY THINK THEY'RE THE TOUGHEST IN THE COUNTRY) — GREAT EFFORT — GREAT TEAM SPIRIT & PRIDE.

"NO ARMY IS AS POWERFUL
AS AN IDEA WHOSE TIME
HAS COME."

MEN OF NOTRE DAME . . . . RISE UP FOR
YOUR FINAL CHALLENGE!

The Phantom

FINAL
NOTRE DAME – 24   MIAMI (FLA) – 22

1968

NOTRE DAME VS OKLAHOMA
9/21/68, GAME #1

"THE PHANTOM SPEAKS"

NO ONE KNOWS THE HEIGHTS OR DEPTHS OF
ACHIEVEMENT THAT CAN BE REACHED WITH "EMOTION."
THE GAME OF FOOTBALL IS PHYSICAL CONDITIONING AND
WE HAVE THAT! IT IS ALSO STRATEGY AND YOU HAVE
THAT! IT IS LASTLY EMOTION OR "HEART." OURS MUST
BE SUPERIOR; IT MUST BE THE KNOWING, ACHING DRIVE
OF THE CHAMPION. WE MAY OF OCCASION BEEN BOWED
. . . ONLY FOR A PLAY OR TWO . . . BUT MENTALLY
NEVER BEATEN.

OKLAHOMA IS "FAST!" LIGHTENING-LIKE QUICKNESS
AND SWARMING TACTICS ARE THEIR TRADEMARKS. THEY
EXPECT THAT NOTRE DAME WILL BE BIGGER AND SLOWER.
THEY KNOW THAT NOTRE DAME WILL BE GREEN AND YOUNG.
MANY OF OUR PLAYERS WILL BE ENTERING THEIR VERY
FIRST COLLEGIATE GAME . . . IN FRONT OF NEARLY
60,000 PEOPLE. LACK OF EXPERIENCE IN SUCH A
"TUMULT" CAN MAKE ANYONE "AWE STRUCK" UNLESS HE
KNOWS WITHIN HIMSELF THAT HE CAN & WILL PERFORM:
THAT NOTHING ELSE MATTERS FOR 60 MINUTES BUT THE
OPPONENT ON THAT FIELD.

WE ARE NOT STRANGERS OR LONELY IN A CROWD THAT
DAY . . . WE ARE ONE IN UNITY, IN FAITH, IN
DESIRE, IN EFFORT! OUR GOAL IS TO WIN AS WELL AS
WE CAN. THERE IS NOT OFFENSE OR DEFENSE ON GAME
DAY . . . THERE IS ONLY A NOTRE DAME TEAM — SOUND
— WITH GREAT EFFORT — WITH ONE UNIFIED THOUGHT &
DIRECTION. GIVE YOUR FULL EFFORT TO PREPARE —
THINK — FULL INTERVAL — THINK — NO BREAKING POINT!
A TEAM THAT REFUSES TO BE OUT-HUSTLED, OUT-DESIRED,
CANNOT BE BEATEN. THIS STARTS TODAY!

B E A T   T H E   S O O N E R S ! ! !

The Phantom

FINAL
NOTRE DAME – 45   OKLAHOMA – 21

1969

NOTRE DAME VS NORTHWESTERN
9/20/69, GAME #1

"THE PHANTOM SPEAKS"

THE "ATMOSPHERE" OF WINNING IS ONE OF HIGH
EXCITEMENT - - - A GREAT UPSURGENCE OF ENTHUSIASM,
PRIDE, - - - - SPIRIT - - - - A COMING ALIVE, AND
A COMING TOGETHER. WE MUST NOW START AWAKENING TO
THE GREAT CONCEPT OF <u>NOTRE DAME TEAM</u>.

IT MUST MEAN HALFBACK OR GUARD, OFFENSE OR
DEFENSE, - - - NOTHING REALLY MATTERS BUT TEAM.
BONDED TOGETHER WE ARE STRONG. WE CANNOT BE BEATEN,
BECAUSE WE REFUSE TO ACCEPT IT.

NORTHWESTERN — STRONGER THAN EVER BEFORE —
REVENGE-MOTIVATED — HUNGRY FROM PRIOR LOSING
SEASONS, WILL TEST THE EXTENT OF OUR OWN HUNGER.
THEY WILL STRIVE TO BREAK US. WE CANNOT HAVE A
BREAKING POINT! WE - - - - HAVE CONDITIONED OUR
<u>MINDS</u> FOR STRATEGY - - - - WE HAVE TAXED OUR
<u>BODIES</u> FOR ENDURANCE AND TOUGHNESS - - - NOW WE
MUST PLAY WITH THE ONE THING THAT SEPARATES THE
NEAR GREATS FROM THE REAL <u>GREATS</u>. WE MUST PLAY WITH
A <u>FULL</u> N O T R E   D A M E   H E A R T.
B E A T   N O R T H W E S T E R N !!

The Phantom

FINAL
NOTRE DAME – 35   NORTHWESTERN – 10

NOTRE DAME VS PURDUE
9/27/69, GAME #2

"THE PHANTOM SPEAKS"

THE MARK OF A <u>GREAT COMPETITOR</u> IS TO COME FROM
BEHIND. AGAINST NORTHWESTERN CIRCUMSTANCES CAUSED
YOU TO DO THIS. WE WERE CEMENTED IN ONE DESIRE
- - - & ONE GOAL - - - & REALLY NO ONE EVER
STRAYED FROM THAT END - - - TO BEAT THEM.
<u>CONGRATULATIONS!</u>
PURDUE - - - DOWN THERE - - - WILL BE QUITE
ANOTHER CHALLENGE . . . OUR JOB IS TO GO DOWN
THERE SO POSITIVE & SO SPIRITED AND SO UNIFIED THAT
IN TRUTH - - - "<u>NO ADVERSITY CAN CHANGE OUR
COURSE.</u>" IT IS ALWAYS A GAME OF BREAKS & MANY
BREAKS ARE MADE.

WE CANNOT — FUMBLE! WE CANNOT BLOW OFFENSIVE &
DEFENSIVE ASSIGNMENTS. WE CANNOT TURN THE BALL OVER
BY INTERCEPTIONS, WE CANNOT BE PENALIZED! THE GAME
WILL GO TO THE TEAM THAT BECOMES THE "<u>HITTERS.</u>" IT
WILL NOT BE A SOFT TASK - - - BUT IT CAN BE DONE
- - - SET YOUR MIND - - - AND IN TURN EVERY TEAM
MIND WILL THINK & ACT & DO - - - THE POSITIVE
THOUGHT OF WORK - - - & EVENTUALLY WINNING OVER
PURDUE! <u>TO THINK "LOSS" IS FOR LOSERS</u>. TO <u>THINK</u>
"<u>WIN" IS FOR WINNERS</u>. "<u>OH YE OF LITTLE FAITH</u>"
REFERS TO ANYONE WHO WANTS WITH JUST NORMAL
INTENSITY - - - BUT TO STRONGLY DESIRE - - - TO
WORK TOWARD A GOAL - - - TO CONSTANTLY DWELL ON
THE END RESULT OF YOUR GOAL - - AND BE WILLING TO
FIGHT FOR IT IS <u>GREAT INDIVIDUAL FAITH</u>. MULTIPLY
THIS BY THE NUMBER OF SQUAD MEMBERS.

<u>THIS FAITH</u>, - - IF HELD AND WORKED WITH - - -
NEVER DOUBTING - - - CAN "MOVE MOUNTAINS"! - - -
CAN "<u>WALK ON WATER</u>" FOR EVEN THE GOOD LORD WROTE
"<u>GREATER THINGS THAN THIS SHALL YOU DO.</u>" THE
MEANING IS CLEARLY TO SET A GOAL — WORK & EXPECT
RESULTS. NEVER, NEVER, NEVER - - - DOUBT THE
OUTCOME! THE <u>DOUBT</u> IS THAT WHICH WEAKENS!

SET YOURSELVES TO UPSET THE BOILERMAKERS IN

```
THEIR OWN BACKYARD - - - - WE'RE GOING DOWN TO GET
THE JOB DONE - - - THAT'S ALL THERE IS TO IT!
                    D O    I T !!!
```

The Phantom

FINAL
NOTRE DAME – 14   PURDUE – 28

NOTRE DAME VS MICHIGAN STATE
10/4/69, GAME #3

"THE PHANTOM SPEAKS"

AS BADLY AS A GREAT COMPETITOR HATES TO LOSE, BECAUSE HE IS A GREAT COMPETITOR HE CANNOT DWELL ON ANY LOSS. A NEW CHALLENGE, ONE THAT GIVES US A CHANCE TO REVENGE A FORMER HEARTBREAK, NOW FACES US.

MICHIGAN STATE HAS A HISTORY OF PLAYING "SOUPED UP" AGAINST THE IRISH, BUT THEY ARE ALSO CAPABLE OF MAKING FUNDAMENTAL MISTAKES. THIS GAME WILL NOT BE A PLACE FOR THE TIMID - - - FOR THEY WILL CHALLENGE YOU OPENLY. WE HAVE A SAYING - - - "THAT NO GAME IS AS IMPORTANT AS THE ONE YOU ARE PLAYING." THIS GAME IS ALL OF THAT!! PREPARE SOUNDLY, WORK HARD - - - BE TOUGH & HARDNOSED - - - NEVER BACKING OFF. THEY WILL ATTEMPT ANY METHOD AT FORCING A CRACK IN YOUR FAITH - - - OR EFFORT. THE ONLY WAY TO BEAT THEM IS THRU A COMPLETE SELLOUT MENTALLY & PHYSICALLY FOR 60 MINUTES. NEVER BACKING UP — NEVER "PLAYING SCARED" - - - WE MUST OUT-HUSTLE - - - OUT-HIT - - - OUT-HEART, MICHIGAN STATE.

THERE IS NO REASON WE CANNOT WIN IF WE DEDICATE OURSELVES TO THAT END. NOT <u>BOYS</u> BUT MEN OF NOTRE DAME, RISE UP.

The Phantom

FINAL
NOTRE DAME – 42   MICHIGAN STATE – 28

NOTRE DAME VS ARMY
10/11/69, GAME #4

"THE PHANTOM SPEAKS"

WHAT HAD FORMERLY BEEN SPARKS IGNITED INTO FULL-GROWN FLAMES OF DESIRE FOR MEMBERS OF NOTRE DAME'S TEAM. UNLIKE ANYTIME I HAVE BEEN ABLE TO RECALL, WE WERE CEMENTED IN A GREAT BOND OF "WE CAN & WE MUST." NOT ONCE DID WE APPEAR IN DOUBT OF OUR ABILITY TO OVERCOME THE SPARTANS. THE WEEK WAS CHARGED WITH EFFORT THROUGHOUT PRACTICE. OUR STRATEGY WAS ONLY EQUAL TO OUR EXECUTION - - - & THAT WAS MAGNIFICENT.

AND NOW - - - - BEWARE OF POST BIG WIN - - - "LET DOWNS." IF IT IS TRUE THAT NO GAME IS AS IMPORTANT AS THE ONE YOU ARE PLAYING - - - ARMY RIGHT NOW IS THAT GAME. WE CANNOT LOOK AHEAD & WE CERTAINLY CANNOT LOOK BEHIND. THE ENTIRE EASTERN SEACOAST WILL WAIT TO SEE THE "IRISH" PERFORM.

PLAY WITH THE SAME ALL-OUT EFFORT & WE CAN BE TOO TOUGH FOR ANYONE TO HANDLE. WE CAME OF AGE - - - BUT DON'T LET "COMING OF AGE" BECOME "RIPE." ARMY HAS GREAT TRADITION, GREAT SPEED, HUSTLE, & HEART. THEY WILL - - - BE UPSET-MINDED. YOU HAVE WORKED TOO HARD TO ALLOW ANY TEAM TO ROB YOU OF YOUR ABILITY THROUGH "LET DOWN."

A VERY WISE MAN ONCE SAID QUITE CLEARLY THAT THE "TRULY GOOD NEVER THINK THEY ARE." THEY WORRY OVER THEIR PROGRESS & TAKE STEPS OF CORRECTION AND ALLOW THE OPPONENT MORE CREDIT THAN IS DUE. - - IF THE TRULY GOOD NEVER THINK THEY ARE - - - - THEY ALSO BELIEVE THAT NO ONE CAN OUTDO THEM.

WIN OVER ARMY - - - - THIS GAME HAS PRODUCED NATIONAL RECOGNITION TO INDIVIDUALS & TEAMS - - - FROM THE CAUSE OF MERELY ONE PLAY.

YOU NOW SHOULD KNOW DEEPLY THE <u>FUN</u> FROM WINNING - - - I DON'T & YOU DON'T WANT TO HAVE IT ANY OTHER WAY.

FINAL *The Phantom*

NOTRE DAME – 45   ARMY – 0

NOTRE DAME VS SOUTHERN CALIFORNIA
10/18/69, GAME #5

"THE PHANTOM SPEAKS"

I KNOW A SECRET TO BEAT SOUTHERN CAL! MY KNOWING IT WON'T GET IT DONE - - - BUT MY TELLING YOU WILL START THE WEEK'S WORK TO ACCOMPLISH THAT GOAL — BEATING SOUTHERN CAL. ALL BIG TASKS START WITH THE IDEA OF WHAT MUST BE DONE - - - THEN THE PREPARATION - - - THEN THE EXECUTION.

THE IDEA IS HERE BECAUSE THIS IS OUR BIG GAME! THE PREPARATION WE CAN ACCOMPLISH! THE EXECUTION WILL BE THE SECRET. IT MUST BE DONE WITH A HUNGRY HEART - - - AN ANGRY HEART - - - AN OVERWHELMING EFFORT. NOT SINGLY, BUT BY THE ENTIRE TEAM. IT CANNOT BE A MON — TUE — WED — THURS — FRI DESIRE - - - BUT ALL OF THOSE DAYS AS ALWAYS - - - & THEN SATURDAY. "THE RISING UP" TO THE FEVER PITCH, THE "SKY HIGH" OF TRUE INTENTION, THE BELIEF THAT WE WILL DO IT BY BEING IRREPRESSIBLE.

NOTHING — NO PLAYER OR PLAYERS CAN WITHSTAND THIS KIND OF SURGE. OUR PLAYERS ON DEFENSE MUST CLAW & DIG & SWARM - - - GANG-TACKLING WITH AN AGGRESSIVENESS NOT YET SEEN ON A FOOTBALL FIELD. THEY MUST CAUSE — PUNTS & FUMBLES & INTERCEPTIONS.

OUR OFFENSE — MUST ROOT PEOPLE OUT OF THE BLOCKS — HARD-NOSE THEM INTO BACKING OFF. OUR RECEIVERS MUST RUN PATTERNS & FIGHT FOR THE BALL. OUR BACKS MUST BECOME "FLAMING DESIRE" INCARNATE.

THIS WILL WIN FOR US - - - THIS GAME MUST COME FROM THE HEART OF PLAYERS - - - - - - NOTHING CAN STOP US - - - OUR HEART, — OUR ATTITUDE.

THIS IS A SECRET - - - KNOWN BY MOST, BUT CARRIED BY FEW. NOTRE DAME MEN - - - RISE UP & EACH PLAYER MAKE THAT PERSONAL VOW THAT SAYS TO HIMSELF, "I WILL GIVE MY BEST EFFORT" — WHOLESALE — SELLOUT SHOT AT GREATNESS. WE CANNOT BE DENIED!!
BEAT SOUTHERN CAL

The Phantom

FINAL
NOTRE DAME – 14   SOUTHERN CALIFORNIA – 14

NOTRE DAME VS TULANE
10/25/69, GAME #6

"THE PHANTOM SPEAKS"

OUR SITUATION IS THIS. WE HAVE ONE LOSS, ONE TIE - - - AND OBVIOUSLY FEEL A BIT DRAINED OF EMOTION AFTER A SUPERB EFFORT VS SOUTHERN CAL. WITHIN OUR REACH IS AN OUTSTANDING SEASON, BECAUSE WE ARE CAPABLE OF BEATING EVERY OPPONENT.

OUR PROBLEM WILL BE THIS. <u>TULANE</u> - - - IN THE HEAT - - - TULANE IN THE SOUTH - - - TULANE IN THE ROLE OF HEAVY UNDERDOG. WE WILL BE WALKING INTO A HORNET'S NEST. ANY TEAM THAT CAN COME FROM A 22-POINT DEFICIT - - - MUST HAVE IMMENSE PRIDE. THE NATURAL REACTION OF OURS - - - COULD BE A - - LET DOWN - - -.

THIS - - - WE MUST NOT LET HAPPEN ELSE ALL WE'VE WORKED FOR THUS FAR IS TARNISHED BEYOND HELP.

THE 2ND HALF OF THE SEASON IS SIMILAR TO THE 2ND HALF OF A GAME. THOSE THAT TIRE - - - THOSE THAT FALL AWAY FROM THEIR BEST EFFORT - - - CAN BE BEATEN.

LET US REGROUP OUR ENERGY - - - AND RE-ESTABLISH THAT — NO GAME OR TEAM IS AS IMPORTANT AS THE ONE YOU ARE PLAYING. THIS WEEK TULANE - - - IN THE HEAT - - - UNDER LIGHTS - - - WITH HOSTILE ENVIRONMENT.

SHAKE OFF ANY DOLDRUMS. WE DID NOT LOSE TO S. CAL. WE MUST HOLD OUR HEAD UP - - - AND FIGHT AS NOTRE DAME'S 1969 TEAM — FIVE MORE TIMES ONLY!!! IT WILL GO TOO QUICKLY - - - & WE CAN NEVER RELIVE THESE OPPORTUNITIES AGAIN - - - LET'S MAKE EACH GAME - - A WORK OF ART.

BEAT TULANE.

The Phantom

FINAL
NOTRE DAME – 37   TULANE – 0

47

NOTRE DAME VS NAVY
11/1/69, GAME #7

"THE PHANTOM SPEAKS"

CONGRATULATIONS ON YOUR WIN OVER TULANE. THE FEAR I PERCEIVE IS OF THE TEAM THAT YOU ARE "SUPPOSED TO BEAT." NAVY IS HAVING A DOWN YEAR - - BUT LAST WEEK - - - THEY WON. THEY ARE SMALLER - - - BUT QUICK. THEY ARE HUSTLERS - - - WELL DISCIPLINED AND EAGER TO HIT. <u>DON'T</u> ONCE FORGET THAT THEY WILL ENTER THE CONTEST WITH EVERY THOUGHT OF WINNING. THEY WILL COME AFTER YOU — - - WITH A "SHOOT THE WORKS - - HOLD NOTHING BACK - - - WE CAN ONLY GAIN" ATTITUDE. THE ONLY WAY TO KEEP WINNING IS TO FIGHT EACH OPPONENT OFF WITH THE SAME FIRED-UP INTENSITY.

THE TRUE CHAMPION - - - DISCOUNTS ALL PREVIOUS RECORDS - - - ALL ODDS PLUS OR MINUS - - - ALL CLIPPINGS, ALL - - - HEARSAY! HE TAKES THE FIELD KNOWING THE OPPONENT IS TRYING TO STEAL A VICTORY FROM HIM. WE CANNOT LET UP IN PRACTICE — IN PREPARATION, OR IN THE GAME.

TALENTED TEAMS ARE UPSET EVERY SATURDAY BY A LESS CAPABLE FOE WHO IS <u>MORE READY</u> TO PLAY.

OUR GOAL IS TO GO ALL THE WAY - - - THEY BAR OUR PATH. BEAT NAVY - - - THERE ARE 2 MORE OPPORTUNITIES FOR OUR SENIORS TO APPEAR ON NOTRE DAME'S TURF . . .

THE DAYS ARE FLEETING, MAKE OF THEM - - - YOUR BEST EFFORT ALWAYS.

THERE IS NO GAME MORE IMPORTANT THAN <u>NAVY</u> THIS WEEK.

The Phantom

FINAL
NOTRE DAME – 47   NAVY – 0

NOTRE DAME VS PITTSBURGH
11/8/69, GAME #8

"THE PHANTOM SPEAKS"

AGAINST NAVY, THE DEFENSE WAS SUPERB. "THEY TAKE A LOT OF PRIDE IN WHAT THEY DO" - - - - CONTINUE!

THE OFFENSE RAN UP A LOT OF YARDAGE, BUT THE FUMBLES AND LACK OF HUSTLE TO THE LINE SHOWED A COMPLACENCY. THIS MUST END!

WE ARE 3 WEEKS AWAY FROM HAVING A SPLENDID SEASON - - - IF WE CAN WIN THE 2 AWAY GAMES AND THE LAST TIME ON THE NOTRE DAME TURF VS AIR FORCE. THOSE TWO GAMES OF GA. TECH AND AIR FORCE DON'T COUNT A LICK - - - BECAUSE PITT IS THE NEXT OPPONENT. NEXT TO SOUTHERN CAL AND PURDUE, THEY ARE THE BIGGEST TEAM WE PLAY. THEY ARE COMING ON AND APPEAR SOLIDLY COACHED. THEY WILL NOT BEAT THEMSELVES. WE CANNOT HELP THEM BY LACK OF HUSTLE, FUMBLES, AND INTERCEPTIONS.

AT PITT, AFTER A BIG WIN OVER SYRACUSE - - - THEY WILL BE OUT TO MAKE THEIR SEASON. ONLY WINNING CAN KEEP US ON TOP. WE NEED TO STAY THERE IF WE WANT TOP RANKING - - - IF WE WANT THE FUTURE REWARDS OF THE VICTORS. WHATEVER WE DO AT PITT - - - LET US NOT BE GUILTY OF FUNDAMENTAL BREAKDOWNS OR LACK OF HUSTLE. THIS IS A CRIME THAT ONLY THOSE WHO ARE NOT GREAT COMPETITORS DARE REPEAT. LET THIS NAVY GAME HAVE TAUGHT US A LESSON. FOOTBALL IS A GAME OF MENTAL AWARENESS - - - FANTASTIC "ATTENTION" AND DEDICATION. IF YOU CANNOT PLAY WITH THE GREAT LOVE AND FIRE NOTRE DAME ASKS FOR - - - SAY SO AND WE WILL FIND A TRUE COMPETITOR.

ALL OF US HAVE BEEN - - BUT WE RELAXED. LET THE LESSON ALLOW YOUR CORRECTION AND DO NOT FALTER THE REST OF THE WAY.

ISOLATE A THOUGHT IN YOUR MIND — NO GAME IS AS BIG OR IMPORTANT AS THE PITT GAME. IF YOU THINK NOT - - HOW WOULD YOU FEEL IF WE ROLLED OVER AND DID NOT WIN? NO ONE - - NO ONE - - CAN ROB US OF

VICTORY IF WE MENTALLY, PHYSICALLY, AND <u>EMOTIONALLY</u>
REFUSE TO LET IT HAPPEN.

The Phantom

FINAL
NOTRE DAME – 49   PITTSBURGH – 7

NOTRE DAME VS GEORGIA TECH
11/15/69, GAME #9

"THE PHANTOM SPEAKS"

CONGRATULATIONS ON THE WIN OVER PITT. OUR
DEFENSE WAS NOT "UP IN THE BIT" - - - BUT THEY
PLAYED WELL ENOUGH TO WIN. BETTER THAN THIS AND
THEY WOULD HAVE HAD A SHUT OUT. OFFENSIVELY WE DID
SOME PRETTY SOUND THINGS, BUT NORMALLY SPEAKING - -
- WE "MOVED" THE BALL WHICH IS THE SECRET TO
OFFENSE.

GA. TECH AT ATLANTA AT NIGHT — THEY HAVE LACKED
LUSTER IN THEIR PREVIOUS TWO GAMES. THE WORD IS
THAT THEY CANNOT SALVAGE THEIR SEASON AT THIS POINT
- - - UNLESS THEY UPSET NOTRE DAME. BY THIS TIME,
THIS SHOULD NOT BE NEW TO YOU.

WE KNOW THEY ARE CAPABLE BECAUSE THEY HAD
SOUTHERN CAL ON THE ROPES WITH LESS THAN 3 MINUTES
TO PLAY - - - WE CANNOT OVERLOOK ANY TEAM SKILLED
ENOUGH TO DO THAT.

OUR LAST GAME AT GA. TECH - - - THEY THREW BEER
BOTTLES, CALLED US DAMNED YANKEES, SPEARED US - - -
TOOK US LATE AFTER A PLAY - - - BUT WE BEAT THEM
IN THE SCORE. THAT IS THE LAST WORD — THERE IS NO
RECOURSE TO THAT!

REMEMBER THAT EACH WEEK IS A NEW WEEK AND A NEW
OPPONENT — ANYTHING CAN HAPPEN TO ANY TEAM ANYTIME!

WITH ONLY 10 DAYS LEFT IN OUR 1969 SEASON WE
ARE TWO MORE VICTORIES AWAY FROM HAVING A GREAT
SEASON. PUSH ON - - - WORK HARD - - - GET MORE
SOLID, MORE AND MORE AWARE. MANY RUMORS OF A BOWL
GAME FILL THE AIR - - - "WHERE THERE IS SMOKE - -
- THERE IS FIRE." WE MUST WIN - - - IF WE ARE EVEN
TO GET A BID TO ONE. IF WE DO NOT - - - THEN AT
LEAST WE - - - CAN REST THRU THE POST SEASON IN
THE KNOWLEDGE THAT WE DID ONE "HELLUVA" JOB.

OTHER TEAMS ARE PHYSICALLY HURTING - - -
DEPRESSED - - - TORN WITH INNER DISSENSION. OUR
TEAM HAS WARDED OFF THIS TYPE OF "CANCER" BECAUSE
WE LUMPED OUR LOYALTY TO WIN. WINNING IS THE
UNITING CAUSE! IT IS A LOT OF FUN TO WIN - - LET'S

GO ON AND WIN OVER GEORGIA TECH - - - BEAT GEORGIA
TECH, DEMOLISH GEORGIA TECH.

THAT - - - EVERYBODY UNDERSTANDS! GO - - IRISH
- - - THIS IS THE STRETCH DRIVE WHERE JACKASSES
FOLD, BUT THOROUGHBREDS PULL IN THEIR GUTS FOR A
FINAL EFFORT OF GREATNESS!!

The Phantom

FINAL
NOTRE DAME – 38   GEORGIA TECH – 20

NOTRE DAME VS AIR FORCE
11/22/69, GAME #10

"THE PHANTOM SPEAKS"

EACH SEASON AND ULTIMATELY EACH GAME AND LASTLY
EACH PLAY OF A GAME, HAS THE POSSIBILITY OF
BECOMING A "WORK OF ART." GAMES WE HAVE WON ARE
WORKS OF ART, HOWEVER, MUCH INDIVIDUAL PLAY HAS
BROKEN DOWN. NOW IT ALL BOILS DOWN TO ABOUT 85
OFFENSIVE AND DEFENSIVE PLAYS IN ONE GAME TO FRAME
THE WHOLE SEASON. THE "MASTERPIECE" THAT CAN BE
- - - CAN ALSO BECOME A SMEARED IMAGE. AIR FORCE
IS THE OBSTACLE IN OUR PATH. THEY ARE A HIGHLY
SKILLED OFFENSIVE MACHINE — LIGHTNING FAST AND
HEAVILY GIFTED WITH INDIVIDUAL SPEED. DEFENSIVELY
THEY ARE ALERT & QUICK, WITH MUCH MORALE AND MUCH
SPIRIT. THEY WILL COME AFTER NOTRE DAME WITH ALL
SYSTEMS GO!.
  NOW I PUT IT TO THE SENIORS - - THE ONES THAT
ARE HANGING UP THEIR NOTRE DAME CLEATS - - - NEVER
TO PERFORM IN OUR GREAT STADIUM AGAIN. I ASK ORIARD
& POSKON, SCHUMACHER & LAWSON, AND KENNEDY AND
RILEY, BRENNAN, ZIEGLER, MCCOY, OLSON, AND GASSER.
WOULD IT NOT BE FITTING THAT ALL OF YOU RISE UP TO
A FINAL GREAT EFFORT? WOULD IT NOT BE A FOND
MEMORY TO REMEMBER THAT AFTER ONLY ONE FAULTY STOKE
OF THE BRUSH - - - OUR PAINTING TOOK ON
PERFECTION?
  THE YEAR OF 1969 - - - THE SENIOR YEAR OF YOUR
NOTRE DAME SQUAD CALLS UPON YOU FOR A GREAT
PERFORMANCE. OUR PLAYING YEARS PASS ALL TOO
QUICKLY. "MAKE OF YOUR LAST COLLEGIATE HOME GAME"
- - - A WORK OF ART. LET US BE SPIRITED, LET US BE
ON FIRE WITH GREAT ENTHUSIASM, HEART & HUSTLE. LET
US CLOSE OUT THE WAY WINNERS SHOULD ALWAYS CLOSE
- - - AS WINNERS!!
  TO THE UNDERCLASSMEN - - IT IS ALSO PART OF
YOUR CAREER, PART OF A SELF-PORTRAIT IN WHICH YOU
EXIST - - - STAND UP & BE COUNTED AS A "HARD NOSE"
— "A FIGHTING HEART" "A WINNER" - - - - WE MAY
NEVER PASS THIS WAY AGAIN. OR ASK YOURSELF - - -

IF IT IS NOT A GREAT TRUTH THAT "WE BECOME WHAT WE DO." WE MUST <u>DO</u> ALL THE THINGS IT TAKES TO BEAT <u>AIR FORCE</u> & THEN WE WILL HAVE BECOME TRUE ARTISTS FOR A JOB WELL DONE. . . IT WILL BE OURS TO SHARE WITH <u>OURS</u> – – – NO ONE CAN EVER TAKE IT AWAY. BEAT AIR FORCE WITH A FULL NOTRE DAME HEART! MAKE THE 1969 FIGHTING IRISH A MEMORABLE GROUP OF MEN.

The Phantom

FINAL
NOTRE DAME – 13   AIR FORCE – 6

1970

NOTRE DAME VS NORTHWESTERN
9/19/70, GAME #1

"THE PHANTOM SPEAKS"

THERE IS A GREAT TRUTH - - - NOT MANY PEOPLE REALLY <u>KNOW</u> IT. MANY ARE AWARE OF IT, BUT CANNOT <u>KNOW</u> IT BECAUSE THEY CANNOT ACCEPT ITS IMMUTABLE POWER. THIS TRUTH CAN GOVERN OUR SEASON, OUR LIVES, OUR VERY PERSON. SIMPLY STATED IT IS THIS: <u>ENERGY FOLLOWS THOUGHT</u>.

THIS IS CERTAIN, THIS IS THE NATURAL FORCE OF LIFE. CALL IT THE "SELF-IMAGE" ONE HOLDS OF ONESELF OR "PSYCHO CYBERNETICS" OR "POSITIVE THINKING," BUT KNOW THIS - - - YOU CAN CONTROL YOUR ENERGY, DIRECT IT, MAGNIFY IT AND FOCUS IT, BY THINKING.

WHAT SHOULD YOU THINK?

THINK THAT WE ARE A TEAM SO DEDICATED, SO BOUND TOGETHER WITH SPIRIT, SO WELL-CONDITIONED, SO STRATEGICALLY READY, SO MENTALLY RIGHT - - - THAT WE ARE A TOTAL FORCE THAT DOESN'T EVER HAVE TO LOSE.

GET A MENTAL PICTURE IN YOUR MIND'S EYE WHAT YOU WISH TO BE AND HOW YOU WANT TO PLAY. ADD TO IT THE FINAL OUTCOME YOU DESIRE. HOLD THESE THOUGHTS — DWELL ON THEM, AND YOUR ENERGY WILL FLOW TO THOSE VERY ENDS.

IF YOU THINK YOU CAN - - - YOU CAN! YOU BECOME WHAT YOU DO, SO DO THOSE THINGS THAT TIE TO THE THOUGHTS YOU WANT TO BECOME REALITY! THINK <u>POWER</u> — THINK <u>SPEED</u>, THINK <u>REACTION</u> — THINK <u>WIN</u> — THINK <u>POSITIVE</u> — AND NEVER ALLOW A SEED OF DOUBT TO CREEP INTO THE POWER BANK OF YOUR GUIDING FORCE - - - YOUR MIND.

ALL GREAT ATHLETES AND GREAT ATHLETIC TEAMS EMPLOY THIS - - - ALTHOUGH MOST OF THEM ARE NOT SERIOUSLY AWARE OF IT. IT WORKS WITHOUT THEIR CONSCIOUS KNOWLEDGE. IT WILL WORK QUICKER AND MORE EFFECTIVELY IF WE ARE AWARE. WHAT I AM SAYING IS THIS. WE MUST HOLD THOUGHTS OF IDEALISM - - - SUCH AS NO ONE TEAM MEMBER WILL EVER <u>LET UP</u> — <u>LOAF</u> — <u>NOT GIVE HIS BEST</u>.

WITH A FULL FORCE OF EFFORT, - - - WITH GREAT
TEAM PRIDE AND COOPERATION, WITH GOOD MORALE - - WE
WILL BE UNBEATABLE!

ALL ENERGY FOLLOWS THOUGHT. IF THE THOUGHT IS
GOOD, THE ENERGY IS FOCUSED IN THAT DIRECTION. ALL
DEEDS REQUIRE ACTION AND ENERGY IS ACTION ON THE
MOVE. BEAT — NORTHWESTERN'S WILDCATS.

The Phantom

FINAL
NOTRE DAME – 35   NORTHWESTERN – 14

NOTRE DAME VS PURDUE
9/26/70, GAME #2

"THE PHANTOM SPEAKS"

NOTRE DAME WILL BE OUTSIZED BY THE PURDUE
BOILERMAKERS! IF SIZE WERE ALL - - - ELEPHANTS
WOULD RULE THE WORLD.

CAN PURDUE — OUT-HUSTLE — OUT-HEART — OUT-HIT
- - - NOTRE DAME? I THINK NOT IF WE PREPARE WELL
AND KEEP THESE THINGS IN MIND:

WE MUST PLAY A POSITIVE GAME, ONE THAT STATES
BOLDLY - - - WE ARE BOUND TOGETHER - - - NOT AS
INDIVIDUALS, BUT AS MEMBERS OF A TEAM. TRY HOLDING
A TOOTHPICK IN YOUR FINGERS - - - SNAP IT IN HALF
- - - EASY? TAKE ELEVEN TOOTHPICKS - - - NOW TAKE
22 - - -. OBVIOUSLY STRENGTH COMES FROM UNITY. WE
ARE NOT TOOTHPICKS BY ANY STRETCH OF THE
IMAGINATION. WE SHOULD BE 22 STOUT-HEARTED AND
ABLE-BODIED PEOPLE - - - SO FULL OF DESIRE AND
HEART & EFFORT THAT PURDUE'S FORCE CANNOT POSSIBLY
COPE WITH OUR FORCE.

FORCE IS AN IDEA - - - IT IS PREPARATION OF
MIND & BODY - - - IN ADVANCE - - - AND THEN
EXECUTION DURING THE TIME OF THE CONTEST.

I DON'T BELIEVE IN JINXES. PEOPLE WHO DO ARE
WEAK-WILLED. I BELIEVE THAT "YOU BECOME WHAT YOU
DO." YOU MASTER YOUR OWN SHIP. REFUSE TO ACCEPT IT
OTHERWISE. WE ARE GOING AFTER THEM WITH A FULL
HEART - - - WITH FULL EFFORT.

WE'RE NOT THINKING OF PERCENTAGES PAST OR FUTURE
- - - JUST THEM & US - - - ON THE FIELD SATURDAY.

GREAT THOROUGHBRED HORSES HAVE AN AIR ABOUT
THEM. LESSER HORSES WITH GREATER SPEED <u>LOSE</u> TO THE
THOROUGHBREDS BECAUSE "HORSEFLESH" YIELDS TO
EXPECTANCY. THEY THINK THEY SHOULD LOSE - - - SO
THEY DO!

I'M NOT AWED BY PURDUE - - - DON'T ANY OF THE
PLAYERS BE - - - RESPECT THEM - - - BUT HOLD THE
IDEA THAT WE CAN AND WILL BEAT THEM - - - & WE'RE
NOT BACKING OFF. THEY'VE MADE THEIR REPUTATION ON
US - - - TELLING EVERYONE HOW "SKY HIGH" THEY GET

FOR THE IRISH BECAUSE THEY LOVE TO BE THE SPOILERS.

TO BE HONEST, WE HAVEN'T PLAYED WELL AGAINST
THEM. I THINK THEY COUNT ON THAT. WHAT A SHOCK
. . . WE CAN GIVE THEM BY BEING MORE THAN READY
- - BY BEING - - - - - NOTRE DAME TO THE FULLEST
MEASURE.

BEAT PURDUE BECAUSE THE WORST THING YOU CAN DO
THE OPPONENT IS SHOW HIM THE SCOREBOARD AT THE
GAME'S END. THIS WE OWE THEM!!! DINARDO - - KELLY
- - TEAM!! RISE — UP!!

The Phantom

FINAL
NOTRE DAME – 48   PURDUE – 0

NOTRE DAME VS MICHIGAN STATE
10/3/70, GAME #3

"THE PHANTOM SPEAKS"

ON SATURDAY SEPT. 26TH THE NOTRE DAME TEAM
EXPERIENCED GREAT <u>PRIDE</u> - - - & <u>SPIRIT</u> & <u>EMOTION</u>.
THEY DISCOVERED "<u>OTHERNESS</u>" AND THE THRILL OF
<u>WINNING</u> OVER AND OLD FOE. WE WERE "ONE" - - -
SATURDAY — UNSTOPPABLE — UNRELENTING — UNBENDING IN
SEEKING OUR GOAL. THAT IS AN EXPERIENCE THAT ALL
SHOULD TREASURE.

TREASURE IT — BUT DON'T LINGER ON IT FOR
SATURDAY, SEPT. 26TH IS A PAGE OF HISTORY — GONE &
- - - OVER WITH - - - HISTORY. NOT ONE PLAY OF THE
PURDUE GAME CAN AFFECT ANY PLAY VERSUS MICHIGAN
STATE.

THE MICHIGAN STATE SPARTANS HAVE PLANS - - -
ALSO: VERY HIGH NOTRE DAME MUST PLAY ON ARTIFICIAL
TURF. THEY ARE ALSO RIDING HIGH ON A HUGE VICTORY
OVER PURDUE. THEY HAVE NOT BEATEN US AT HOME - - -
SINCE 1949. THEY ARE RIPE FOR A LET DOWN. ALL
TEAMS HAVE LET DOWNS AFTER EMOTIONAL UPRISINGS.

THIS IS THEIR PLAN - - - THEIR HOPE! SOUTHERN
CAL RELAXED & GOT TIED 21 — 21. MISSOURI TOOK
LIGHTLY - - - AN AIR FORCE TEAM & LOST. PENN STATE
RELAXED AFTER AN EASY WIN AND & GOT PASTED. THE
STAGE IS SET, IS IT NOT? THE PATTERN IS THERE
- - - NO ONE REALIZES THAT IT HAPPENS - - - YOU
CAN'T FEEL YOURSELF RELAX OR RIPEN OR LET UP - - -
OR LOSE INTENSITY. AFTER ALL, SHOULDN'T PLAYERS
RELAX AFTER A BIG WIN? SHOULDN'T MICHIGAN STATE
ROLL OVER AND PLAY DEAD BECAUSE OF THE MIGHTY
IRISH? JUST A LITTLE RELAXING WON'T HURT - - -
AFTER ALL A LITTLE IS JUST A LITTLE - - BUT
MAGNIFY & MULTIPLY A LITTLE TIMES 22 AND YOU HAVE
A <u>LOT</u>, OR ENOUGH TO CAUSE UPSETS!!

THERE IS ONE POINT THAT IS OF <u>GREAT SIGNIFICANCE</u>
& UTTER <u>IMPORTANCE</u>. THIS IS "<u>FOREWARNED</u>." ALTHOUGH
BEING AWARE OR FOREWARNED IT NOT ALWAYS "FOREARMED"
IT IS THE ELEMENT OF SAFETY AGAINST AN UPSET. TEAMS

WHO LIVE IN THE PAST — WALK TOO TALL - - & SPEAK
TOO LOUD - - - & WORK TOO LITTLE, ARE FAIR GAME.

OUR THIRST TO WIN — OUR HUSTLE - - - OUR
KNOWLEDGE OF HOW MICHIGAN STATE WILL COME AFTER US
WITH GREAT REVENGE - - - SHOULD ALARM EACH OF US.
THEY WILL FIGHT US IN THEIR BACK YARD. WE'VE COME
FAR - - - WE CAN GO STILL FURTHER - - - BUT CANNOT
AFFORD THE LUXURY OF WALKING INTO A HORNET'S NEST
AT EAST LANSING WITHOUT KNOWLEDGE OF WHAT IT WILL
BE LIKE. EXPECT THE ROUGHEST PHYSICAL GAME. IT WILL
TAKE ALL OF THIS KNOWLEDGE — ALL OF OUR WORK —
EFFORT & PREPARATION TO WIN. GO - IRISH!! THIS
SEPARATES THE MEDIOCRE FROM THE GREAT.

FOR GREATNESS IS CONSISTENCY OF EFFORT - - PRIDE
& EXECUTION.

IT IS NEVER RELAXING BECAUSE THE "CHAMPION" IN
YOU RISES UP ANEW & DOES NOT RECOUNT OLD BATTLES
UNTIL THE ENTIRE WAR IS OVER.

BEAT MICHIGAN STATE!!

The Phantom

FINAL
NOTRE DAME – 29   MICHIGAN STATE – 0

NOTRE DAME VS ARMY
10/10/70, GAME #4

"THE PHANTOM SPEAKS"

THE NOTRE DAME FOOTBALL TEAM OF 1970 HAS GROWN
INTO A SOLID FORCE - - - A RUGGED UNIT. PHYSICALLY
THEY WILL RETAIN CONDITION, STRATEGICALLY THEY WILL
BE ABREAST OF OPPONENTS. THE LAST FACET IS THE ONE
TO BE FIRMLY GUARDED. "BEING MENTALLY READY" TO
PLAY.

UNQUESTIONABLY YOU CANNOT BE "SUPER-CHARGED" FOR
EVERY OPPONENT. THERE ARE DAYS THAT WE MUST BE
SUPER-CHARGED. THERE ARE NO DAYS, HOWEVER, WHEN YOU
CAN RELAX. THERE IS NO OPPONENT & NO GAME THAT YOU
CAN TAKE LIGHTLY. EACH PREPARES FOR YOU. EACH PRAYS
& PLANS TO UPSET YOU. EACH HOPES TO GET YOU ON THE
"OFF DAY" THE "FLAT PERFORMANCE" THE "RIPE STAGE."

TO COMBAT THIS YOU MUST REMEMBER & STUDY THIS
PHRASE: "NO GAME IS AS IMPORTANT AS THE ONE YOU
ARE GOING TO PLAY." NO GAME REALLY IS - - - JUST
THE ONE AT A TIME THAT YOU MUST PLAY. THIS WEEK
- - - ARMY!! ARMY IS SMALLER - - - LIGHTER - -
QUICKER - - MORE DISCIPLINED - - MORE EMOTIONAL
- - MORE SUPER-CHARGED THAN THE AVERAGE OPPONENT
WILL BE. THEY COME TO OUR HOME - - - WITH NOTHING
TO LOSE AND EVERYTHING TO GAIN. THEY WILL BE READY.
MAKE NO MISTAKE ON THAT ACCOUNT.

EVEN FRIENDS & RELATIVES UNKNOWINGLY FALL INTO A
TRAP. THEY, AS ALL OUTSIDERS, THINK AND SAY THIS
IDEA WITH PERHAPS SLIGHTLY DIFFERENT PHRASING.
"ARMY - - YOU GUYS SHOULDN'T HAVE ANY TROUBLE WITH
ARMY!!" STANFORD MUST HAVE FELT THAT WAY AGAINST
PURDUE!!

THE GAME, HOWEVER INTRICATE IT MAY GET, IS STILL
BLOCKING & TACKLING, HUSTLE & PRIDE - - -. WHAT
YOU DID ANOTHER DAY AGAINST ANOTHER TEAM IS OF NO
REGARD - - - IF WE ARE TO CONTINUE WINNING!

KNOW THIS & KNOW IT WELL: IT IS A SLIGHT SLIP &
SHORT TRIP FROM THE "PENTHOUSE TO THE OUTHOUSE."

ARMY IS AN OPPONENT - - WHO SEEKS TO ROB YOU OF

YOUR HARD-FOUGHT GAINS. THEY WANT TO GAIN THE
PRESTIGE OF THEIR SEASON AT YOUR EXPENSE.

CHAMPION PLAYERS & CHAMPION TEAMS DO NOT ALWAYS
GO TOGETHER. THE CHAMPION PLAYER IS AN INDIVIDUAL.
THE CHAMPION TEAM IS ALWAYS A UNIFIED FORCE,
CONSISTENT — DEPENDABLE FOREVER COMPETITIVE —
THEREIN LIES THE GREATNESS OF CHAMPION TEAMS - - -
CONSISTENCY!

WE HAVE A GREAT START NOTRE DAME OF 1970
- - - - LET'S NOT UNDO ALL THAT WE HAVE ALREADY
DONE.

BEAT ARMY!!

The Phantom

FINAL
NOTRE DAME – 51   ARMY – 10

NOTRE DAME VS MISSOURI
10/17/70, GAME #5

"THE PHANTOM SPEAK"

"THERE IS A TIME AND A PLACE FOR EVERYTHING
- - - A TIME TO LIVE AND A TIME TO DIE."
A TIME TO PLAY <u>SUPER-CHARGED</u> AND A TIME TO <u>RENEW</u>
DEDICATION. — WE PLAYED ARMY — FLAT - - - WITH
LITTLE EMOTION - - - FORGOT TECHNIQUES, BLEW
ASSIGNMENTS, LACKED HUSTLE. — WE WERE NOT HUNGRY TO
PLAY & HUNGRY TO WIN! THE TIME TO PLAY IS THE GAME
TIME! WE VIOLATED THIS PRINCIPLE - - - WE'RE VERY
LUCKY - - - WE WON AGAINST A PHYSICALLY INFERIOR
TEAM.

DESPITE ALL FOREWARNING - - - DESPITE DISCUSSION
& REMINDER - - - WE ALL LET UP A LITTLE. MAYBE
HUMAN NATURE DEMANDED THAT WE BE SO AFTER PURDUE &
MICHIGAN STATE WHERE RAW EMOTION FLOWED FREELY.

AND NOW - - - - AND NOW - - - MISSOURI — TWICE
BEATEN — PHYSICALLY QUICK — STRONG — UPSET-MINDED
HAS US IN THEIR BACKYARD - - -.

TO WIN THIS GAME COULD MAKE US 5 & 0 WITH A
WEEK REST TO REGROUP & FINISH STRONG. WITHIN OUR
GRASP IS "GREATNESS." OURS NOT FOR THE ASKING BUT
<u>FOR</u> THE <u>DOING</u>.

THE TIME FOR DOING - - FOR HUSTLE — FOR PRIDE —
FOR TECHNIQUE — FOR EMOTION — FOR <u>SUPER-CHARGED</u>
EFFORT IS AGAINST MISSOURI.

INJURIES HAVE NICKED US BUT EACH MAN CAN SUCK IN
HIS GUTS AND GO A LITTLE TOUGHER, A LITTLE HARDER
— TO TAKE UP THE SLACK.

WHEN IS THE TIME? - - - THIS WEEK IS <u>ONE OF</u>
<u>THOSE TIMES</u> - - - FOR MISSOURI IS NOT ARMY. THEY
WILL BE FAR SUPERIOR — BETTER SKILLED & PERHAPS THE
QUICKEST TEAM WE WILL PLAY.

WE HAVE AN OPPORTUNITY THAT LIFE OFFERS FEW
PEOPLE - - - WE HAVE A SHOT AT "GREATNESS." BUT IF
EVERYTHING OF WORTH IS BOUGHT ONLY WITH <u>PAIN</u> &
<u>SACRIFICE</u> - - - - IMAGINE WHAT YOU MUST INVEST TO
WIN <u>GREATNESS</u>. SELL — OUT! GET READY! RISE UP! LIVE
WITH THE DEDICATION THAT SAYS "I WILL IMPROVE — I

WILL BE A GREAT CONTACT PLAYER - - - I WILL ADD A
DIMENSION TO THE TEAM BY MY EXTRA EFFORT!"

THERE IS NO BACK-PEDALING - - - NO WAY TO STOP
TIME. WE CAN STOP HERE, — CONTINUE HALF HEARTEDLY,
— OR GO ON <u>OUR WAY</u>, ALL THE WAY! IF WE <u>DECIDE</u> TO
PAY THE PRICE.

AND REMEMBER THIS — <u>DESIRE IS PRAYER</u> — <u>PRAYER IS</u>
<u>FORCE OF THOUGHT</u>. TO DESIRE & PRAY & THINK & WORK
AT AN IDEA IS TO ULTIMATELY SEE IT BECOME REALITY.
WITHIN OUR GRASP IS A REAL SHOT AT BEING WHAT WE
WANT TO BE. "<u>WANTING</u> TO" IS 50% OF ALL SUCCESS.
"<u>WORK</u>" IS THE OTHER.

<u>BEAT MISSOURI</u>!!

The Phantom

FINAL
NOTRE DAME – 24   MISSOURI – 7

NOTRE DAME VS NAVY
10/31/70, GAME #6

"THE PHANTOM SPEAK"

WHEN YOU THINK ABOUT FOOTBALL AND PIT ONE TEAM
AGAINST ANOTHER, IT IS EASY TO LOSE SIGHT OF AN
UNDENIABLE TRUTH. BOTH TEAMS FIELD THE SAME NUMBER
OF PEOPLE.

THE ELEVEN THAT NAVY WILL PUT ON THE FIELD DON'T
HAVE YOUR RECORD - - - YOUR NAME - - - YOUR
"FAVORITE'S ROLE." THEY ARE EQUAL TO NOTRE DAME IN
SIZE. THEY ARE JUST AS QUICK. THEY "IN OTHER WORDS"
ARE CAPABLE OF KNOCKING OFF NOTRE DAME. THAT IS THE
UNDENIABLE TRUTH.

WHAT PREVENTS UPSETS? INTENSITY DOES - - - BEING
READY TO PLAY - - - KNOWING THE UNDENIABLE TRUTH &
BEING JUSTIFIABLY CONCERNED.

. WE SIT 5 & 0 - - - AND NAVY IS AN OBSTACLE IN
OUR PATH TO THE GOAL WE'VE SET. ANY SUCCESS THAT
THEY HAVE ON OFFENSE OR DEFENSE, ANY BREAK WE GIVE
THEM THRU AN INTERCEPTION, PUNT RETURN OR FUMBLE -
- - GIVES THEM RAW FUEL & BUILDS THEIR "<u>BELIEF</u>"
THAT THEY CAN WIN. CONVERSELY - - - IF WE ARE
SOUND ON OFFENSE - - - MAKING FEW ERRORS - - -
MAKING SUSTAINED DRIVES WITH NO TURNOVERS; IF WE
ARE SOUND ON DEFENSE — HARD HITTING & INTENSELY
INVOLVED WITH BEATING THEM . . .

WE CAN PLAY THEM & BE 6 & 0! IF WE REALLY STOP
TO ANALYZE WHAT HAS HAPPENED - - - YOU'LL KNOW
THAT WE HAVE PAID DEARLY FOR EVERY VICTORY WITH
MUCH EFFORT. THAT TOO IS AN UNDENIABLE TRUTH. YOU
CAN'T <u>WIN</u> IF YOU DON'T PAY THE PRICE.

OUR TEAM — OUR GROUP OF MEN - - - THEIR LOYALTY
- - - THEIR BOND - - - THEIR EXECUTION IS BASED ON
THE STRENGTH OF MEN NOT STRONGER THAN OTHER
INDIVIDUALS BUT STRONGER IN THE <u>UNITED EFFORT</u>, THE
TEAM CONCEPT - - - THE GOAL OF WINNING. THAT IS
EXACTLY WHAT SEPARATES WINNERS FROM LOSERS.

IF YOU LIKE THE IDEA OF WINNING, KNOW THAT
SUCCESS IS FICKLE - - - IT LEAVES ONE IF INTENSITY
DWINDLES!

GO AFTER NAVY BECAUSE AT THIS POINT & ON THAT
DAY - - - NO TEAM & NO GAME IS AS IMPORTANT TO US
THAN NAVY.

THEIR QUICKNESS — THEIR MILITANT DISCIPLINE —
THEIR WILL TO WIN WILL BE HIGH & READY. AFTER ALL
- - - THEY'RE ELEVEN WILL SHOW UP AND THEY DON'T
JUST PLAN TO GO THROUGH THE MOTIONS. EACH DAY &
EACH GAME, THE PAST BECOMES HISTORY. IT WILL BE A
BRAND NEW NAVY THAT FACES US - - - - - BUT
REMEMBER THIS, NOTRE DAME HAS THE KNOWLEDGE OF ALL
OF THIS - - - NOTRE DAME IS US, THE PEOPLE WHO
ASSUME THE IDENTITY WHILE REPRESENTING H E R ! WE,
TOO, WANT TO WIN.

WANT TO BEAT NAVY - - - WANT TO GET #6 - - -
BEAT NAVY.

The Phantom

FINAL
NOTRE DAME – 56   NAVY – 7

NOTRE DAME VS PITTSBURGH
11/7/70, GAME #7

"THE PHANTOM SPEAKS"

SIX-TENTHS OF THE NOTRE DAME SEASON IS OVER. WE
ARE 6 & 0. IT WAS RUMORED THAT NAVY WAS NOT A BIG
GAME - - - I HEARD A PERFECT ANSWER THAT IT WAS
THE MOST IMPORTANT GAME - - - AFTER ALL IF YOU
LOSE - - IT BECOMES THAT, THE MOST IMPORTANT GAME.
OUR OPPONENT THIS WEEK IS PITTSBURGH. IT IS OUR
MOST IMPORTANT GAME.
A WORD OF CAUTION - - - PURDUE, BADLY BEATEN BY
NOTRE DAME, FACED STANFORD - - - STANFORD LOOKING
AHEAD ONE WEEK TO SOUTHERN CAL PLAYS "DEAD" &
LOSES. YES, THEN THEY BEAT SOUTHERN CAL THE NEXT
WEEK - - - BUT TO WHAT AVAIL. A WIN IS A WIN - - -
A LOSS IS A LOSS! LIKE BEING PREGNANT - - - THERE
IS NO IN-BETWEEN - - - YOU ARE OR ARE NOT WINNERS!
PITTSBURGH LOOKED AHEAD - - - FIGURING SYRACUSE
WAS NOTHING - - - BUT JUST THINK AFTER SYRACUSE WE
GET THE "IRISH." THEY LOOKED FOR US ON THE WEEK
BEFORE WE PLAYED THEM. IT COST THEM, BUT THEY WILL
BE READY FOR US - - - DOUBLY SO BECAUSE OF THE
LOSS. A WORD ABOUT THE PANTHERS: IN PREVIOUS YEARS,
WE HAVE TAKEN THEM APART RATHER BADLY. THEY HAVE A
NEW COACH. HE HAS RECONSTRUCTED THEIR BELIEF IN
THEMSELVES.
MAN FOR MAN THEY ARE BIG! THEY HAVE SCORED ON
EVERYONE. THEY OVERCAME A 30-POINT DEFICIT IN ONE
HALF AGAINST WEST VIRGINIA TO BEAT THEM IN THE 4TH
QUARTER.
WHAT I'VE SAID IS THEY HAVE SIZE - - - BELIEF
IN THEMSELVES - - - WON'T QUIT - — & HOLD REVENGE
FOR NOTRE DAME. EVERY REASON GOING FOR THEM TO COME
IN HERE SUPER-CHARGED!
IF WE ARE 6/10THS OF THE WAY HOME - - - AND
EACH OPPONENT GETTING TOUGHER - - - WE DO HAVE ONE
BREAK. WE PLAY HERE AT NOTRE DAME 3 TIMES IN A
ROW. WE HAVE OUR HOME CROWD TO PERFORM FOR - - - -
WE HAVE OUR PERSONAL PRIDE AND OUR SENIORS TO FIGHT
FOR. WE ARE MAKING THE STRETCH TURN IN THE RACE;

THE ONE WHERE THOROUGHBREDS HAVE "SOMETHING" LEFT
TO SPURT THROUGH THE CROWD.

PITTSBURGH WILL NOT BE AN EASY GAME. WE MUST BE
SOUND! WE CANNOT FUMBLE OR HAVE INTERCEPTIONS. WE
CANNOT MISS ASSIGNMENTS OR DO THEM POORLY. AND
LASTLY - - - WE MUST OVERWHELM THEM WITH OUR BEING
CHARGED - - THEY ARE ATTEMPTING TO <u>STEAL</u> WHAT WE
HAVE WORKED TOO HARD FOR. PLAY WITH A FULL NOTRE
DAME HEART. BECAUSE WE ARE WITHIN STRIKING DISTANCE
OF COLLEGE FOOTBALL IMMORTALITY. IT WILL CHANGE
YOUR LIFE.

BEAT PITT!

The Phantom

FINAL
NOTRE DAME – 46   PITTSBURGH – 14

NOTRE DAME VS GEORGIA TECH
11/14/70, GAME #8

"THE PHANTOM SPEAKS"

GEORGIA TECH - - - GEORGIA TECH! THEY ARE COMING
NORTH TO PLAY THEIR <u>BOWL GAME</u>! REMEMBER THE BEER &
POP CANS THEY THREW AT US - - THE PILING ON, THE
SPEARING OF HELMETS - - THE FOUL TREATMENT OF THEIR
SOUTHERN HOSPITALITY OF A YEAR AGO. REMEMBER THAT
WE PLAYED THEM DOWN THERE AND THERE WAS NO WARM
WATER TO SHOWER AFTER - - THAT THEIR FANS SPIT AT
US & RIDICULED OUR PLAYERS & STAFF - - - &
REMEMBER TOO THAT THE WORST THING YOU CAN EVER DO
TO A TEAM IS TO BEAT THEM ON THE SCOREBOARD!!

THEY ARE TOUGH — THEY ARE EXCEPTIONALLY <u>QUICK</u> —
THEY HAVE BEEN WINNERS - - - THEY WILL BE
ELECTRICALLY CHARGED. THIS WILL BE THEIR SEASON'S
HI-LITE.

WE WERE NOT REALLY CHAMPING AT THE BIT VERSUS
PITTSBURGH. WE CAUGHT A SCARE - - REGROUPED & CAME
BACK - - -EVERY TEAM GETS UP FOR THE IRISH.
GEORGIA TECH WILL BE UP! EVERY TIME WE HAVE PLAYED
THEM, THEY HAVE TIRED TO HURT SOMEONE PHYSICALLY
- - - THEY WERE ROTTEN HOSTS. WE ARE NOW HOSTING
THEM — LET US BE KIND & CONSIDERATE & MEEK &
HUMBLE - - - FOR AFTER ALL, NO TREATMENT AFFECTS
THE SCORE. W H A T YOU D O O N T H E F I E L
D D O E S ! !

DON'T STRAY AN INCH - - - DON'T LISTEN TO
WOULD-BE DETRACTORS ABOUT "LSU" & "SOUTHERN CAL" &
WHICH "BOWL" BEING BIG IMPORTANT GAMES.

IS THERE ANY GAME MORE IMPORTANT THAN THE ONE
YOU ARE TRYING TO WIN?? HELL NO!! WE HAVE TO KEEP
ON KEEPING ON — TAKING ONE AT A TIME. 3 BIG SURGES
OF EFFORT & SPIRIT & CRACKLING ENTHUSIASM — SURE,
BUT DON'T THINK IN <u>THREE</u>. THINK ONE AT A TIME!

OUR SCOUTS SAY GA. TECH IS A SOLID — QUICK —
TOUGH — GOOD, SOUND FOOTBALL TEAM & THAT WE MUST
PLAY A TOUGH PHYSICAL & MENTAL GAME TO WIN. WE
HAVE ALWAYS STATED THINGS AS THEY ARE; & THAT'S HOW
THEY ARE!

WE'VE COME A LONG HARD WAY. WE'VE BANDED
TOGETHER - - - WE'VE HELPED & ENJOYED ONE ANOTHER'S
SUCCESS. WE HAVE NOT BEEN SELFISH & WE ARE TRULY A
TEAM. WHAT KEEPS US FROM BEING A <u>TRULY</u> <u>GREAT TEAM</u>
IS THE NEXT OPPONENT. HE BARS OUR WAY.

DEFENSE - - - CALLED SLOW & UNENTHUSED BY THE
SOUTHERN SPEEDSTERS (S W A R M!) (THEY HAVE THE
FASTEST HB-PUNT RETURNER & K.O. RETURNER EVER).

OFFENSE - - - HAS BEEN CALLED A BIG CUMBERSOME
LINE & SLOW STUMBLING BACKS, R I S E   U P !
LET'S PUT IT ON THE LINE 3 MORE TIMES & - - - THE
FIRST OF THESE AGAINST GA. TECH. NEVER LET A LACK
OF GREAT DESIRE RUB AGAINST YOU. BE SMART ENOUGH TO
KNOW THAT WE ARE KNOCKING FOR A SLICE OF GREATNESS
THAT ONLY A RARE FEW HAVE HAD A CHANCE AT.

R I S E   U P   &   B E A T   G A.   T E C H!

The Phantom

FINAL
NOTRE DAME – 10   GEORGIA TECH – 7

NOTRE DAME VS LSU
11/21/70, GAME #9

"THE PHANTOM SPEAKS"

SATURDAY AGAINST GA. TECH, THE DEFENSE PLAYED SUPERBLY WITH THE EXCEPTION OF ONE PLAY.

THE OFFENSE WAS <u>SLIPSHOD</u> — <u>NO SUSTAINED EFFORT</u>, <u>MISSED ASSIGNMENTS</u>, <u>SOMETIMES LACK OF HUSTLE</u>. <u>IT WAS THE OFFENSIVE TEAM'S POOREST PERFORMANCE</u>! IN ALL - - - AND THRU ALL — - WE STILL WON. AFTER GA. TECH BE ALERTED!

OUR SCOUTS SAY LSU IS THE FINEST DEFENSE THEY HAVE EVER SEEN IN COLLEGE FOOTBALL! THEY HAVE NOT HAD A TOUCHDOWN SCORED ON THEM ON THE GROUND THE ENTIRE SEASON.

FOR A SOLID YEAR THEY HAVE LOOKED FORWARD TO NOTRE DAME CRYING, "THE TIGERS ARE GOING TO GET YA!"

THEY CLAIM NO ONE CAN PLAY DEFENSE BETTER THAN LSU. THE REPORT OF THE SCOUT IS - - - - NO ONE REALLY KNOCKS ANY OF THEIR PEOPLE <u>OFF</u> THEIR FEET. THEY PURSUE, THEY GANG-TACKLE. NOTRE DAME COULD NOT POSSIBLY HAVE THAT KIND OF DEFENSE - - - AS FOR NOTRE DAME'S VAUNTED OFFENSE - - - "HELL" — "GA. TECH" STIFLED THEM.

DINARDO IS GONE FOR THE SEASON! THIS IS THE LAST TIME SENIORS WILL EVEN PLAY IN THE NOTRE DAME STADIUM!

IT WILL TAKE A <u>SUPER-CHARGED</u> EFFORT TO BEAT LSU.

THINK OF LARRY DINARDO PLAYING THE WHOLE GAME VIRTUALLY ON ONE LEG. IF EACH PLAYER SWELLS HIS HEART TO "DINARDO" SIZE, IF EACH PLAYER SUCKS IN HIS GUTS A LITTLE TIGHTER, IF EACH SENIOR MAKES HIMSELF RESPONSIBLE TO "JERK UP" HIS TEAMMATES FOR A SUPER-CHARGED EFFORT - - - WE CAN WIN!! IF YOU WANT TO BE "CHAMPIONS" WE MUST WIN THE GAME! THE CHALLENGE IS THERE! THEY SAY THEY PLAY BETTER DEFENSE THAN ANYONE — THEY SAY ALSO THAT NO OFFENSE CAN DENT THEM. THEY STRESS PUNT RETURNS, KICK OFFS, AND SELL-OUT FOOTBALL. THEY HAVE PREACHED "NOTRE DAME" FOR ONE WHOLE YEAR.

ON THE OTHER HAND, DWELL ON THIS THOUGHT. "A TEAM THAT WON'T BE BEATEN, CAN'T BE BEATEN." HOW DO YOU <u>WON'T</u>? WELL, YOU SAY TO YOURSELF, I WON'T BE LAZY! I WON'T MISS AN ASSIGNMENT! I WON'T GIVE UP! I WON'T BE DENIED! - - - I WON'T SETTLE FOR LESS THAN VICTORY!

YOU THINK ABOUT IT — YOU WORK AT IT - - -. YOU GIVE IT A MAN-SIZED ATTENTION SPAN WITH A MAN-SIZED EFFORT - - - & WE COMBINE & RISE UP - - - & SWELL UP TO A PEAK HIGHER THAN WE HAVE EVER BEEN - - - TO LSU.

BEAT LSU ON THE FINAL GAME OF NOTRE DAME'S HOME SEASON.
BEAT — LSU!

The Phantom

FINAL
NOTRE DAME – 3   LSU – 0

NOTRE DAME VS SOUTHERN CALIFORNIA
11/21/70, GAME #10

"THE PHANTOM SPEAKS"

WHEN THE END OF A LONG HARD PULL NEARS - - - AND
THE FINISH LINE IS IN SIGHT - - MANY A WOULD-BE
CHAMPION HAS NOTHING LEFT WITH WHICH TO FINISH.

ON THE OTHER HAND - - - GREAT RESERVE - - -
ABUNDANT ADRENALIN - - THE NERVE & SINEW OF
CHAMPIONS COMES ON - - - FOR THE FINAL PUSH!

KNOWING THIS NOTRE DAME, WINNING OVER SOUTHERN
CAL AND STRETCHING 9 & 0 TO 10 & 0 ALLOWS NO OTHER
TEAM THE CHANCE TO BEAT THAT RECORD. THEY MIGHT —
WITH GREAT EFFORT, TIE IT - - - BUT IT WILL STAND
FOR ALL TIME! YOU WILL BE THE 1970 TEAM - - - THAT
WENT 10 & 0.

IT WON'T BE EASY! FOR SOUTHERN CAL IS AS GOOD A
PHYSICAL TEAM AS ANYONE. THEY WILL HAVE ONLY ONE
IDEA - - - & THAT IS TO UPSET NOTRE DAME & SAVE
WHAT THEY CAN FOR THEIR SEASON. A WIN CAN'T REALLY
HELP THEIR SEASON, BUT IT WILL MAKE OURS GREAT —
IF WE CAN WIN!!!

EVERY SENIOR - - - EVERY PLAYER TRY PULLING
YOURSELF UP TO YOUR BEST EFFORT.

THE DEFENSE: - - - ROSES FOR YOUR SUPERB EFFORT
VS. LSU!

THE OFFENSE: - - - YOU WON ON DAYS WHEN DEFENSE
NEEDED HELP - - - NOW YOU MUST REGROUP FOR ONE
LAST UNITED EFFORT!

THE 10TH GAME OUT THERE WILL NOT BE AN EASY
CHORE. THEY WILL BE AWAITING US. THEY ARE NOT
UNBEATABLE AS THEY HAVE SEVERAL LOSSES & A TIE WITH
NEBRASKA. FORGET ALL OF THIS, HOWEVER, FOR WHEN WE
ARRIVE, IT WILL BE A NEW GAME.

DEFENSE, CAN YOU DO "LSU" ONE MORE TIME IN 1970?
QUESTION MARKS TO THE OFFENSE. CAN YOU BOUNCE BACK
& REDEDICATE???? YOU ARE TIRED — DRAWING TO A CLOSE
OF A LONG, HARD PULL — - DOES THAT. WE ARE SO
CLOSE TO FINISHING UP SUCH A GREAT SEASON, WE
CANNOT GIVE IT UP — GUT UP!!

EVERY MEMBER OF THIS TEAM CAN BE A MEMBER OF THE 1970 NATIONAL CHAMPION GROUP!

WE MUST REDEDICATE OURSELVES - - - FIND FRESH FAITH - - - <u>NEW</u> SPIRIT - - <u>NEW</u> CONFIDENCE IN OURSELVES AND COME OUT FIGHTING: NOT UPTIGHT, BUT <u>HARD</u> & <u>EAGER</u> TO PERFORM & WIN! IT IS ALL IN FRONT OF US - - - WITHIN OUR GRASP - - - <u>LACK</u> OF EFFORT OR DESIRE SHOULD NOT EVER STOP US! LASTLY - - - SOUTHERN CAL IS NEW THE MOST IMPORTANT GAME!!!! THERE IS NO GAME SO IMPORTANT! THERE IS NO DEFENSE FOR THE ONSLAUGHT OF GREAT EFFORT & ENTHUSIASM. THESE ARE TOOLS WE MUST EMPLOY TO BEAT SOUTHERN CAL!

BEAT - - - THEM, BEAT SOUTHERN CAL & FINISH UP THIS BEAUTIFUL WORK OF ART - - THIS UNTAINTED, UNTARNISHED — UNDEFEATED SEASON.

BEAT SOUTHERN CAL!!!

The Phantom

FINAL
NOTRE DAME – 28   SOUTHERN CALIFORNIA – 38

1971

A MESSAGE TO THE 1971 TEAM

"SOME MEN GROW OLD STRIVING TO BE GREAT, TOO BUSY TO PLANT THE SEEDS OF SMALL MOMENTS."

IN EACH OF YOUR LIFETIMES — FOOTBALL IS BUT A GROUP OF SMALL MOMENTS. THE GREATNESS OF LIFE IS COMPRISED OF EXACTLY THE COLLECTION YOU WILL EXPERIENCE. THE SEED WE HOPE TO PLANT, AND SOMEDAY - - HARVEST - - IS THAT OF THE NATIONAL CHAMPIONSHIP!

THE RECIPE FOR SUCCESS - - - THE FORMULA FOR HOPE, IS COMMOM KNOWLEDGE, BUT THE EXECUTION IS FAR MORE DIFFICULT. IT IS WITHIN OUR GRASP — WITHIN A 120-DAY SPAN — WITHIN A DEDICATED GROUP OF SMALL MOMENTS TO ACHIEVE TRUE GREATNESS.

THE INGREDIENTS ARE:

1. ONE BUSHEL OF UNITY: NEVER BACK-BITING, NEVER SECOND-GUESSING, NEVER DOING YOUR OWN THING - - - OWN IS SINGULAR — TEAM OR UNITY IS PLURAL, THAT IS THE SECRET FORCE OF A DISCIPLINED GROUP OF MANY MEN WITH BUT ONE GOAL.

2. ONE BUSHEL OF LOYALTY: THE WILL THAT CAN WARD OFF ANYONE OR ANYTHING THAT WOULD SUPPORT SUBRTRACTING FROM OUR TEAM'S EFFORT.

3. STIR IN GENTLY: 80 TO 100 YOUNG MEN THAT UNDERSTAND LIFE - - - THAT FOOTBALL IS A MEANS TO AN EDUCATION - - - AND ALSO AND EDUCATION SUPERB ON THE FIELD. MEN WHO HAVE THEIR OWN MINDS, BUT ARE UNAFRAID TO ACT IN A SUBORDINATE ROLE FOR THE SAKE OF A WORTHY TEAM GOAL - - - AND ALL VOLUNTARILY ACCEPTING THIS.

4. A CUP OF LEADERSHIP POURED GENTLY THROUGHOUT THE MIX: "IF YOU FOLLOW THE CROWD - - - THE CROWD WILL NEVER FOLLOW YOU." WE MUST SET STANDARDS OF DEDICATION — HARD HITTING — NO BREAKING POINTS. WHAT OTHER CROWDS DO IS OF INTEREST TO FOLLOWERS ONLY.

5. ONE THICK FROSTING OF HUMILITY: THE LAST INGREDIENT FOR GREATNESS IS TO PREPARE WELL - - - GIVING AND TRYING YOUR BEST — NEVER

GIVING QUARTER OR ASKING ONE — WINNING FAIRLY
AND NOT BOASTING OR GLOATING.

PEOPLE SPEAK OF "NOTRE DAME MAGIC." LITTLE DO
THEY REALIZE THAT THE "MAGIC" IS IN THE PEOPLE WHO
PLAY - - - BECAUSE THEY WANT TO — FOR ALL THEIR
WORTH - - - FOR THEY ARE GREAT COMPETITORS — GREAT
HEARTS — THE WORLD KNOW THEM AS "<u>WINNERS.</u>" THE
MAGIC IS <u>SWEAT</u> — HARD WORK AND THE WHOLE OF THIS
FORMULA. IF WE REAP ONLY WHAT WE SOW . . . LET US
BEGIN AND SO WELL!

The Phantom

NOTRE DAME VS NORTHWESTERN
9/18/71, GAME #1

"THE PHANTOM SPEAKS"

MOST PEOPLE HAVE THE <u>WILL TO WIN</u>. ONLY WINNERS HAVE THE WILL TO PREPARE TO <u>WIN</u>.

THIS DAY & THIS WEEK ARE THE BEGINNING — THEY ARE PAGES IN THE BOOK OF YOUR LIFE. HOW WILL THE 1971 IRISH BOOK READ? WILL IT STATE?

1. THEY WERE HARDNOSED & HITTERS!
2. THEY HAD NO BREAKING POINT BEHIND OR AHEAD.
3. THEY PLAYED THE GAME FOR A FULL 60 MINUTES.
4. THEY PLAYED WITH A FULL HEART.
5. THEY WERE NOT INDIVIDUALS, BUT AN INTRICATE WEAVE OF MANY TALENTS DEDICATED TO ONE FINAL RESULT.
6. THEY — HAD — CLASS — POLISH — PRIDE!

IF IT STATES THESE THINGS, IT IS NATURALLY ACCEPTABLE THEY CAN BE CHAMPIONS.

YOU - - - PLAY A GAME - - - ON A GIVEN DAY - - - WITH A GIVEN OPPONENT. SATURDAY THE 18TH, NORTHWESTERN IS <u>THE</u> DAY & THE OPPONENT. NO GAME WILL BE AS IMPORTANT AS THAT GAME THAT DAY.

The Phantom

FINAL
NOTRE DAME – 50   NORTHWESTERN – 7

NOTRE DAME VS PURDUE
9/25/71, THE GAME #2

"THE PHANTOM SPEAKS"

CONGRATULATIONS - - - ON YOUR 1ST BIG WIN AGAINST NORTHWESTERN'S WILDCATS.

THE DEFENSE PLAYED SUPERBLY - - - THEY HELD NORTHWESTERN - - - STALEMATED, AND SCORED TWICE THEMSELVES - - - AN EXCELLENT DISPLAY OF TEAM DESIRE AND "TOGETHERNESS."

OFFENSIVELY — WE STARTED SLOWLY. WE MADE SEVERAL ERRORS, AND WE DID NOT SUSTAIN LONG DRIVES. THIS WE CAN CORRECT. GET BETTER! GET SET! GET CORRECTED THE SMALL ERRORS. BEGIN TO BECOME A <u>UNIT</u>, A SINGLE-MINDED UNIT . . . PERFORMING WITH BUT ONE GOAL - - - TO WIN.

PURDUE — IS BIG - - - THEY ARE QUICK - - - THEY HAVE BEATEN US DOWN THERE - - - ALL TOO OFTEN. LET'S GET READY FOR A HEAD-KNOCKING AFFAIR — - IF YOU ENJOY THE JOY OF WINNING — FORGET LAST SATURDAY, IT IS HISTORY, AND PURDUE IS FUTURE. OUR FUTURE DOWN THERE DEPENDS ON <u>DESIRE</u> — DEDICATION TO DETAIL — ALL-OUT EFFORT AND A FULL 60 MINUTE GAME WITH A FULL HEART. NO MEMBER OF THE TEAM IS MORE IMPORTANT THAN THE TEAM AND NO GAME SO IMPORTANT AS PURDUE. LET'S GO GET THE BOILERMAKERS.

The Phantom

FINAL
NOTRE DAME – 8   PURDUE – 7

NOTRE DAME VS MICHIGAN STATE
10/2/71, GAME #3

"THE PHANTOM SPEAKS"

A THOUSAND TIMES YOU'VE HEARD - - - THE GAME
IS <u>SIXTY</u>, YES <u>60</u> - - - MINUTES LONG - - - NOT <u>ONE</u>
AND NOT <u>59</u>, BUT 60 - - - THE TOTAL PACKAGE!

A MILLION TIMES YOU'VE HEARD THAT IT IS A "GAME
OF INCHES" - - - THAT YOU HAVE "NO BREAKING POINT"
- - - THAT "PRESSING THE KICKING GAME" CAUSES BIG
BREAKS - - - IT ALL HAPPENED SATURDAY - - - WE
WERE LUCKY - - - WE WERE DETERMINED, BUT MOST OF
ALL WE WERE A TEAM! AS MUCH AS YOU WOULD LIKE TO
SAVOR THE WIN, YOU CANNOT. MICHIGAN STATE SHOOK
THEIR DOLDRUMS — GOT NEW MOMENTUM AND FOUND NEW
SPIRIT. THEY WILL COME HERE WITH FIRE IN THEIR EYE.

PURDUE IS NOW HISTORY - - - IT CANNOT HELP US
FROM HERE ON — - GET SET FOR MICHIGAN STATE.

OFFENSE AND DEFENSE - - - MADE ERRORS - - - WE
MUST CORRECT THEM. WE MUST PREPARE AGAIN FOR THE
MOST IMPORTANT GAME OF ALL - - - THE <u>ONE</u> WE ARE
GOING TO PLAY.

WE TOO, SHOULD COME ALIVE - - - NOT HAVING
PLAYED GREAT - - - WE MUST REALIZE OUR MISTAKES
AND ALSO REALIZE THAT "NEVER QUITTING" - - - "NEVER
BACKING OFF" - - - GETTING UP WHEN IT COUNTS - - -
AND NOT BEATING OURSELVES, DRAWS US A LITTLE
TIGHTER. WE'VE WORKED, SWEAT, PLAYED AND WON
TOGETHER. THAT IS THE THRILL OF BEING A TEAM - - -
BUT NONE OF IT COUNTS UNLESS YOU <u>WIN</u> TOGETHER.

<u>OFFENSE</u> — WE MUST FIGHT FOR CONSISTENCY
<u>DEFENSE</u> — WE MUST REGAIN OUR IMPENETRABLE — -
CONCEPT.

<u>TEAM</u> — WE MUST STEADILY IMPROVE. NEVER TAKING
ANY OPPONENT LIGHTLY. NEVER FORGETTING THEY ALL GET
SKY HIGH FOR NOTRE DAME!

SO WHAT ELSE IS NEW?

The Phantom

FINAL
NOTRE DAME – 14   MICHIGAN STATE – 2

NOTRE DAME VS MIAMI (FLA)
10/9/71, GAME #4

"THE PHANTOM SPEAKS"

THERE ARE MANY WAYS TO WIN! AND THAT'S WHAT IT
IS ALL ABOUT! IN THE HEAT - - - IN THE HUMIDITY,
OUR TENACITY. OUR "NO BREAKING POINT" OUR INTENSE
TEAM PRIDE, ACHIEVED OUR 3RD VICTORY. THOUGH WE
WERE NOT SPECTACULAR OFFENSIVELY AND HAD 4 FUMBLES
AND ONE INTERCEPTION, OUR EARLY DRIVES AND OUR
DEFENSIVE UNIT'S SUPERB STANDOFFS ALLOWED US TO
WIN. MANY WAYS TO WIN! - - - BUT WE WIN TOGETHER,
AS A TEAM SHOULD.

MIAMI, FLORIDA — HOT — MUGGY — HUMID - - - AN
AROUSED TEAM - - A COMEBACK TEAM - - - A TEAM THE
SCOUTS PROCLAIM PLAY WITH FANTASTIC ENTHUSIASM &
HUSTLE, WILL BE GOING FOR THE UPSET.

WARNING — <u>DON'T</u> MISJUDGE THEM!!! THEY ARE A GOOD
SOLID TEAM. WE MUST CORRECT OUR ERRORS.

ON OFFENSE: WE WERE NOT HITTING OUT WITH THE
COUNT — WE DID NOT <u>WIN </u>THE LINE OF SCRIMMAGE
CONSISTENTLY. WE <u>FUMBLED</u> FOUR TIMES & HAD ONE
INTERCEPTION. WE CANNOT KEEP ON TURNING THE BALL
OVER TO THE DEFENSE. WE HAVE COST OUR OWN DEFENSE
TWO SHUTOUTS WITH MISPLAYS BY THE OFFENSE.

WE MUST RESOLVE OURSELVES AS A TEAM, THAT WE CAN
TAKE NO ONE LIGHTLY, THAT WE WILL <u>WIN</u> THE SCRIMMAGE
LINE OFFENSIVELY & DEFENSIVELY AND THAT WE WILL
PLAY A FUNDAMENTALLY SOUND GAME FOR A FULL 60
MINUTES. THAT'S WHAT IT TAKES - - - TOUGH TO DO
- - - BUT DOING IT & WINNING IS THE GREATEST FUN
IN THE GAME.

A WISE MAN ONCE SAID - - - "DESIRE" IS PRAYER
- - AND PEOPLE WITH GREAT DESIRE OFTEN FULFILL
THEIR OWN PRAYERS & DREAMS. HAVE GREAT DESIRE.

OUR <u>DREAM</u> OR <u>PRAYER</u> OR <u>GOAL</u> AS A TEAM IS TO BE
THE BEST WE CAN BE; IMPROVING EVERY WEEK, MAKING
FEW MISTAKES AND ULTIMATELY WINNING THE CONTEST. WE
CANNOT BE DISTRACTED FOR A DAY, A WEEK, OR A GAME.
THE ONLY "<u>BIG</u>" GAME THAT COUNTS IS THE ONE TO BE
PLAYED - - - THIS GAME, AT THIS POINT, IS MIAMI,

ON A FOREIGN FIELD - - - UNDER THE LIGHTS — WITH
AN ANTI CROWD, WITH MUCH HEAT, AND FANTASTIC NOISE.
IT WILL TAX US! IF WE HAVE A DESIRE TO KEEP ON
WINNING — TO SHOW POISE & CLASS TO BE & STAY
UNBEATEN - - - WE MUST RISE UP TO THE CHALLENGE.

"WHEN A THOROUGHBRED IS CHALLENGED, HE REACTS
WITH GREAT EFFORT. A JACKASS MERELY REFUSES." THE
CHOICE IS OURS. WE KNOW THE ODDS - - THE SCORE - -
THE SITUATION.

LET'S FIRE UP FOR THE MIAMI HURRICANES & SHOW
THEM WHAT NOTRE DAME REALLY STANDS FOR. THEY CLAIM
WE ARE OVERRATED, THAT PEOPLE ARE IN AWE OF OUR
SIZE OR OUR NAME.

PERFORMANCE MAKES BELIEVERS OF EVERYONE - - -
FATIGUE MAKES COWARDS OF US ALL!

GUT UP - - - PREPARE TO WIN THE MOST IMPORTANT
GAME OF ALL; THE ONE WE ARE GOING TO PLAY VS.
MIAMI!!!!

The Phantom

FINAL
NOTRE DAME – 17   MIAMI (FLA) – 0

NOTRE DAME VS NORTH CAROLINA
10/16/71, GAME #5

"THE PHANTOM SPEAKS"

NOTRE DAME - - - YOU ARE NOW 4 & 0. YOU FACED THE CHALLENGE OF PLAYING AN AWAY GAME - — A GOOD OPPONENT - - - A CHARGED-UP TEAM IN HEAT, ON STRANGE TURF. YOU NEVER BROKE, YOU NEVER LET UP. THE MIAMIANS KNOW WHY WE ARE NOTRE DAME - - - THEY KNOW THAT BEING NOTRE DAME IS NOT AN EMPTY THING. IT MEANS CLASS, - - - IT MEANS GREAT EFFORT, IT MEANS NEVER GETTING SHOOK.

BECAUSE WE ARE NOTRE DAME AND MOST PEOPLE EXPECT SOMETHING SPECIAL, IT ALLOWS EVERY OPPONENT WE PLAY TO BE "EMOTIONALLY HIGH & TRIGGERED" FOR US. THERE IS NEVER A TEAM THAT WON'T BE AT ITS BEST WHEN WE PLAY THEM. IT IS THE HIGHEST COMPLIMENT THEY CAN PAY US - - AND THEY DO IT UNKNOWINGLY.

SOMETHING ELSE THEY ARE UNKNOWINGLY ABOUT IS THIS: WE NEVER TAKE ANYONE LIGHTLY. WE REFUSE TO BE OUT-HIT, OUT-HUSTLED — OUT-HEARTED. WHERE THEY GET SKY HIGH FOR BIG GAMES. WE JUST PLAY EACH GAME HIGH, FOR HIGH IS OUR NORM! BECAUSE NO GAME IS MORE IMPORTANT THAT THE ONE WE ARE GOING TO PLAY. THIS IS THE HALF-WAY MARK. NORTH CAROLINA HAS A SOLID, TOUGH FOOTBALL TEAM. YES, THEY WILL BE HIGH - - - MAYBE THEY LOOKED IN ADVANCE TO US LAST WEEK - - & LOST THEIR FIRST GAME.

WE MUST CONTINUE TO IMPROVE — GIVING FULL ATTENTION & FULL DEVOTION.

LET NOTHING SUBTRACT FROM OUR MOMENTUM — ! — WORK WHEN IT IS TIME TO WORK — ! — RELAX WHEN THERE IS TIME - - - FOR THERE IS A TIME & PLACE FOR EVERYTHING! - - - THE TIME TO WIN IS EACH SATURDAY - - - AND EVERY SATURDAY IS THE BIGGEST GAME OF OUR LIVES - - -THERE IS NO GAME SO IMPORTANT TO US, AS NORTH CAROLINA!

FINAL
NOTRE DAME – 16   NORTH CAROLINA – 0

NOTRE DAME VS USC
10/23/71, GAME #6

"THE PHANTOM SPEAKS"

IN ONE PARAGRAPH — OFFENSE I SAW INDIVIDUAL
EFFORT - - - NO TEAM UNISON. THERE SEEMED LITTLE
SPARK - - NO GREAT TEAM PRIDE. WE WALKED TO THE
LINE OF SCRIMMAGE. WHEN WE EXITED THE FIELD, WE
CANNOT EVEN SIT TOGETHER SOLIDLY TO GO OVER
STRATEGY. IS EVERYONE A PLAYER COACH? CAN'T WE GET
OURSELVES HITTING ON ALL CYLINDERS & REALIZE THAT
ERRORS HAVE KILLED OUR DRIVES? EACH MEMBER HAS HIS
OWN INDIVIDUAL BREAKDOWNS THAT HAVE CONTRIBUTED TO
THIS.

TECHNIQUE — ASSIGNMENT — EXECUTION. THE THREE
THINGS OFFENSE IS COMPOSED OF - - - WE HAVE EACH
AT TIMES, BUT NEVER ALL TOGETHER. OUR ATTITUDE MUST
CHANGE. WE MUST THINK SCORE, THAT WE CAN, THAT WE
WILL, THAT WE MUST. WHAT GOOD IS 600 YARDS OF
OFFENSE OR 6 IF YOU DON'T GET THE ULTIMATE, THE
SCORE? - - - ALL PLAYS IN ANY DRIVE ARE WASTED! WE
WASTED — 83 PLAYS — 83 BLOCKS - - - OF EFFORT, OF
TIME — WASTED.

TO THE DEFENSE - - - WHO PLAYS AS A GREAT TEAM
KNIT — WITH DEEP & INTENSE PRIDE — WITH FIERY
ENTHUSIASM WITH JOY FOR THE SUCCESS OF OTHERS
- - - WITH SPARKLING ENTHUSIASM - - - ROSES
- - - - YOU WERE SUPERB!!

IF — A TWO-LETTER WORD THAT HOLDS ALL THE
ANSWERS TO ALL OF LIFE'S PROBLEMS - - IF THE
DEFENSE CAN MAINTAIN — WHAT IT HAS SHOWN! IF THE
OFFENSE CAN SUDDENLY EXPLODE ITSELF INTO THINGS
THAT IT HAS HINTED AT - - - & IF THE IRISH ARE
ENTITLED TO GET SKY HIGH ONCE IN A WHILE AGAINST
AN OPPONENT - - - - WE CAN BEAT SOUTHERN CAL.

HERE IS THE SITUATION. THEY ARE HAVING A LOSING
SEASON. GOD ONLY KNOWS WHY — BECAUSE THEY ARE THE
TALLEST, HEAVIEST, QUICKEST & MOST TALENT-LADEN
TEAM WE PLAY. THEY HAVE NOT REACHED ABOVE
THEMSELVES TO JELL - - THEY HAVE NOT PLAYED WITH
WILD ENTHUSIASM - - - BUT THEY HAUNT THE IRISH

- - - THEY MOCK THEM — & LAUGH & JEER AT THEM BECAUSE THEY <u>LOVE</u> THE ROLE OF SPOILER. THEY LIE IN WAIT FOR NOTRE DAME - - - THEY WANT THIS UPSET BECAUSE IT IS ALL THEY HAVE LEFT TO SALVAGE THEIR SEASON.

TWO CAN PLAY AT THAT GAME - - - WE <u>OWE</u> <u>THEM</u> <u>SOMETHING</u>. THEY TRIED TO REALLY PUSH OUR NOSES IN THE MUD AT S.C. ONLY OUR WILL NOT TO BREAK PREVENTED IT. WE OWE THEM A "SUPER-CHARGED" GAME. ONCE N A WHILE A TEAM OWES ITSELF A MOMENT OF PEAK PERFORMANCE, A MOMENT OF FLOWING ADRENALIN - - -A MOMENT OF CLIMBING HIGHER & CLAWING HARDER THAN IT EVER THINKS IT CAN. RIGHT NOW GET SET FOR THE DAY OF SOUTHERN CAL - - - DON'T RISE TOO QUICKLY - - - BUT SET YOUR MINDS - - PRACTICE FULLY - - - GET THE WORK POLISHED & ACCOMPLISHED UNTIL THE SAT. OF OCT. 23RD.

NO GAME - - - IS MORE IMPORTANT THAT SOUTHERN CAL!

LET'S SOCK IT TO 'EM!! GREAT ACTION IS CAUSED BY GREAT THOUGHT WHEN COUPLED WITH GREAT EFFORT. RISE UP & REACH OUT FOR A GREAT DAY . . .

The Phantom

FINAL
NOTRE DAME – 14   USC – 28

NOTRE DAME VS NAVY
10/30/71, GAME #7

"THE PHANTOM SPEAKS"

A GREAT WARRIOR FATALLY WOUNDED, BUT NOT YET
DEAD - - - WAS HEARD TO UTTER - - - "<u>A LITTLE I'M</u>
<u>WOUNDED BUT NOT YET SLAIN</u> - - - <u>I'LL BUT LIE DOWN</u>
<u>AND BLEED AWHILE</u> - - - <u>THEN I'LL RISE TO FIGHT</u>
<u>AGAIN</u>!"

THE MARK OF GREATNESS, OF FIBER, SINEW, & HEART
- - - IS ALSO THE RARE & BRILLIANT CAPACITY TO
CAST OFF ADVERSITY - - - TO GO ON UNDAUNTED,
UNBOWED - - - UNAFRAID - - - TO <u>BOUNCE BACK</u>.

WHEN THEY ASK, OF WHAT IS NOTRE DAME MADE? LET
THE ANSWER BE IN OUR ATTITUDE - - - & OUR PHYSICAL
& MENTAL RESPONSE. WE BEAR NO FALSE PRIDE, NOR DO
WE FEEL SHAME. WE GIVE OUR ALL EVERY TIME — WE
BATTLE. THERE CAN BE NO SHAME IN THAT.

A SET OF CIRCUMSTANCES AGAINST A POWERFUL
OPPONENT WHO HAD 4 LOSSES - - STORING THEIR VENOM
- - - THEIR FRUSTRATION FOR THE ONLY THING THAT
COULD SAVE THEIR SEASON. . . . EXPLODED IN OUR
FACES.

WE WERE NOT AT OUR BEST - - - BUT WHERE WE
WERE, WAS NOT GOOD ENOUGH ON THAT DAY.

QUO VADIS? - - - WHERE FROM HERE? CAN WE LICK
OUR WOUNDS - - - RE-GATHER - - - PICK UP THE
PIECES & <u>STORM</u> BACK? THAT TAKES CHARACTER — IT
TAKES CLASS - - IT MEANS CALLING ON A RESERVE
WITHIN ONESELF THAT SAYS TO THE WORLD - - - "I'LL
BE DAMNED IF I'M THROUGH - - - I'M NEVER THROUGH!
THAT WAS A BATTLE - - - NOT A WAR. THE WAR IS THE
ENTIRE SEASON. WE WENT FOR ALL OF IT - - - BUT WE
STILL WANT WHAT IS LEFT.

NOW - - - YOU'LL FIND OUT WHAT WE ARE MADE OF
- - - BY OUR HUSTLE - - - OUR LACK OF DESPONDENCY,
OUR ATTENTION TO DUTY - - - OUR ABILITY TO
SCRAMBLE FROM A KNOCK DOWN & COME BACK WITH THE
HEART OF CHAMPIONS - - -. WE TOOK AN 8 COUNT - - -
A KNOCKDOWN, BUT NOT A KNOCKOUT.

WE HAVE 4 MORE OPPONENTS - - - ONE AT A TIME.

LOOKING BACK IS FOR LOSERS - - - THERE IS NO GAME
MORE IMPORTANT THAN OUR NEXT GAME AGAINST NAVY. WE
CAN NEVER EVER TAKE ANYONE LIGHTLY. NAVY JUST UPSET
DUKE WHO OBVIOUSLY "LOOKED" BY THEM. . . . RATHER
LIGHTLY. DUKE BEAT STANFORD & STANFORD BEAT
SOUTHERN CAL - - - ETC.

WHAT ARE WE MADE OF - - - ? WE ARE MEN MADE OF
PRIDE — MADE OF UNITY — OF FIGHTING HEARTS — LET
US BEGIN AGAIN! LET US START WHERE SUCCESS STARTS
— - AT THE BEGINNING, WITH NEW RESOLVE - - - WITH
GREAT EFFORT, INTENTION, & EXPECTATION; FOR SUCCESS
& FAILURE ARE BOTH FLEETING IMPOSTORS WAITING TO
DUPE ALL WHO GRIEVE OR CELEBRATE. WHAT IS DONE IS
DONE! TOMORROW IS A NEW DAY - - - "FACE IT WITH
GRACE" - - - WITH NEW HOPE & THE NOTRE DAME MAN'S
FACILITY - - - TO RISE AGAIN!

P.S. "FAME IS A VAPOR, POPULARITY AN ACCIDENT,
RICHES TAKE WINGS. THOSE WHO CHEER YOU TODAY WILL
CURSE YOU TOMORROW. ONLY ONE THING ENDURES - - -
CHARACTER." (HORACE GREELEY ON HIS DEATHBED. IT
TAKES CHARACTER TO BOUNCE BACK!)

The Phantom

FINAL
NOTRE DAME – 21   NAVY – 0

NOTRE DAME VS PITTSBURGH
11/6/71, GAME #8

"THE PHANTOM SPEAKS"

PITTSBURGH IS AS BIG AS WE ARE - - - AS FAST - - - AS EAGER. WE ARE IN THEIR STADIUM ON NEW TURF - — IN FRONT OF THEIR PEOPLE! THEY'LL BE UPSET-MINDED. LAST YEAR THEY THREATENED OFTEN. - - THAT IS ENCOURAGING TO THEM - - - IT GAVE THEM FUEL.

DEFENSIVELY WE MUST BE READY TO SWARM, TO SELL OUT, TO BE PHYSICALLY & MENTALLY PSYCHED UP TO DESTROY THEIR OFFENSE.

OFFENSIVELY - - - WE MUST GET THE TIMING — THE CONSISTENCY OF THESE THINGS -. <u>HUSTLE</u> — <u>FIRE OUT</u> — <u>ERROR FREE</u> - - - <u>DRIVE & SCORE</u>!

NO ONE WILL EVER CONVINCE ME THAT THE GREATEST VIRTUE A GREAT PLAYER HAS - - IS SIZE OR SPEED OR TALENT. IT IS PURELY MENTAL DESIRE TO EXCEL — GREAT ENTHUSIASM — GREAT FOCUS OF CONCENTRATION. ALL "MENTAL." YOU BECOME WHAT YOU DO! WE MUST PRACTICE WITH HUSTLE, WITH ENTHUSIASM, WITH EFFORT - - - TO PLAY WITH IT!

EACH MEMBER OF THE OFFENSE MUST TAKE THE RESPONSIBILITY OF HIMSELF SAYING "I DON'T WANT TO BE THE GUY THAT DOESN'T HUSTLE - - - THAT MISSES MY ASSIGNMENT - - - OR DOESN'T GIVE A FULL EFFORT."

WHEN ELEVEN PEOPLE DECIDE THIS & PRACTICE THIS - - - THEN EXECUTION & AWESOME POWER ARE THE RESULTS. THAT'S WHAT WE MUST DO TO WIN. DOMINATE THE OPPONENT — WIN THE SCRIMMAGE LINE - - - ATTACK THEM - - - & BLEED OUT YARDS.

TOGETHER THEN - - - THE OFFENSE MOVING & SCORING - - - ERROR FREE - - - THE DEFENSE GETTING FIELD POSITION, DESTROYING OPPONENT MORALE - - - AND TOTALLY <u>DOMINATING</u> THE GAME - - - WE CAN BEAT PITTSBURGH.

MAKE NO MISTAKE - - - THEIR IDEA IS THE SAME - - - ONLY INDIVIDUAL DEDICATION DISTINGUISHES WHOSE <u>IDEA</u> IS IGNITED & WHOSE WITHERS & DIES. THAT IS WHERE THE "BREAKING POINT" <u>IS</u>!

I SUPPOSE YOU HAVE TO LOSE SOMETHING — TO REALLY
APPRECIATE IT. THESE ARE GREAT DAYS TO BE AN
ATHLETE. YOU PLAY FOR NOTRE DAME ONCE IN YOUR
LIFETIME - - - - ONE SHORT 4-YEAR SPAN - - -
SENIORS HAVE ONLY 3 MORE WEEKS & IT IS OVER.

IF YOU THINK PRACTICE IS DRUDGERY, IF YOU FEEL
TIRED OF THE GRIND, - - IF YOU BEGIN TO WANT IT TO
END & DON'T CARE HOW IT DOES - - - YOU HURT ALL
AROUND YOU! YOU ALSO BECOME A "FOOL" OF TIME - - -
NOT WISE ENOUGH TO KNOW THIS IS "YOUR TIME" - - -
THERE IS NO OTHER - - - WHEN THE SEASON ENDS. — IT
IS OVER. WHAT YOU DO WHEN IT REALLY COUNTS SHOWS
WHAT YOU ARE. THE NEXT 3 WEEKS REALLY COUNT - - -
WORK AT THEM, ENJOY THEM - - - MAKE THEM YOUR BEST
EFFORT . . . & GO BEAT THE PANTHERS.

The Phantom

FINAL
NOTRE DAME – 56   PITTSBURGH – 7

NOTRE DAME VS TULANE
11/13/71, GAME #9

"THE PHANTOM SPEAKS"

<u>WORDS</u> - - - EVERYONE USES THEM - - - FEW PEOPLE
LISTEN TO THEM. YOU WERE TOLD - - - OVER & OVER
AGAIN. THE GAME IS "<u>MENTAL</u>" AMONG OTHER THINGS. YOU
CAN BELIEVE NOW THAT ONE'S MENTAL ATTITUDE CAN
CONTROL ENTHUSIASM — MOMENTUM — PERFORMANCE?

THE (PITT) WAS OUR BEST TEAM EFFORT. WE MOVED ON
OFFENSE — WE SWARMED ON DEFENSE. WE MADE THE
TURNOVER BREAKS - - - & WERE NOT DENIED IN THE
SCORING DEPARTMENT. THAT WAS NOTRE DAME KIND OF
HUSTLE.

WE HAVE TWO BIG GAMES LEFT, BUT AT THIS STAGE
NONE MORE IMPORTANT THAN THE TULANE GAME THIS
SATURDAY.

THEY HAVE BEEN AN UP & DOWN TEAM - - - WITH A
MEDIOCRE SEASON. TEAMS SUCH AS THIS PRESENT A
DIFFICULT PSYCHOLOGICAL BARRIER. FROM OUR
STANDPOINT WE CAN <u>NEVER</u> <u>EVER</u> OVERLOOK ANYONE. FROM
THEIR STANDPOINT - - - THEY WILL MAKE THIS THEIR
BOWL GAME. WHEN YOU ARE EXPECTED TO BE THE UNDERDOG
- - - IT IS EASY TO RISE - - - FOR ANYTHING YOU DO
IS A BONUS.

KNOW THIS! THEY WILL BE AT THEIR BEST FOR NOTRE
DAME. NO GAME OR NO PLAY PRIOR TO THIS GAME WILL
COUNT AN IOTA. THIS - - - NOW IS WHAT COUNTS. WE
MUST FORCE THEM TO THEIR "BREAKING POINT" BY
DOMINATING THEM!

IN THE TAIL END OF LAST SEASON - - WE WERE
TIRED AND INJURED - - - THE PRESSURE OF A LONG
BATTLE AT EACH FRESH NEW OPPONENT'S CHALLENGE —
TRYING TO MAKE ITS REPUTATION ON NOTRE DAME - - -
IT BECAME A LITTLE TOUGH. WE SCORED 10 POINTS IN
OUR 8TH GAME & 3 IN OUR 9TH. OUR DEFENSE HUNG
TOUGH HOWEVER - - - & IT WAS ENOUGH.

WE'VE HAD SLUGGISH MOMENTS THRUOUT 1971 - - -
BUT AN <u>IDEA</u>, A <u>THOUGHT</u> - - - <u>SOME MOMENTUM</u>. <u>SOME</u>
NEW <u>ENTHUSIASM</u> CAN LIFT US TO REALLY MAKE <u>OUR</u> MOVE.

HERE IS WHAT WE MUST DO! WHAT GOOD - - - TO

LEAD THE RACE 3/4 AROUND THE TRACK - - - THE
FINISH IS WHAT COUNTS. WE MUST <u>FINISH</u> STRONG —
VIBRANT — PSYCHED — JUBILANT — UNBENDING —
UNYIELDING — DYNAMICALLY. WE MUST BEAT TULANE
SOUNDLY - - - & FINISH OUR 10TH GAME THE SAME. WE
ARE AT THE STAGE NOW WHERE EVERYTHING CAN HAPPEN -
- - & ALL OF IT IS GOOD IF WE CONTINUE TO WIN.

EVERYTHING A TEAM HAS OR OWNS OR CONTAINS IS
COLLECTIVE - - - IF ALL ARE A TOUCH LAZY - - - YOU
HAVE A TOUCH MULTIPLIED BY THE TOTAL NUMBER & THAT
IS A LOT LAZY.

IF EACH PLAYER FEELS ENTHUSIASM - - - HE
RESPONDS WITH WORK - - - & EFFORT - - - JUST A
LITTLE MORE THAN HE HAS AND IT IS MULTIPLIED BY
THE TOTAL NUMBER OF THE TEAM. WE WILL <u>MUSHROOM</u> OUR
TOTAL QUANTITIES. HOLD THE THOUGHT OF:
"ENTHUSIASTIC WORK" "CONCENTRATED EFFORT"
"TOGETHERNESS" "UNITY" "DESIRE" "<u>PRIDE</u>"

THESE ARE JUST WORDS EVERYONE USES - - - FEW
PEOPLE LISTEN - - - OH TO BE <u>DIFFERENT</u> & <u>TUNED IN</u>
FOR THE SPURT IN THE END OF WHAT COULD BE <u>OUR</u> RACE
- - - <u>TULANE IS THE ENEMY</u>! NO GAME IS MORE
IMPORTANT!

The Phantom

NOTRE DAME VS LSU
11/20/71, GAME #10

"THE PHANTOM SPEAKS"

IF, IN THE PAST YOU HAVE "TAKEN LIGHTLY THE
PHANTOM'S WORDS" - - - YOU WERE TOO SOPHISTICATED
TO KNOW - - - THAT HE MERELY TRIED TO GIVE YOU
INSIGHT & IMPETUS - - - MAKE THIS THE <u>EXCEPTION</u> &
<u>READ</u>.

AFTER MUCH RESEARCH - - - & MANY AVENUES OF
INFORMATION - - - LET ME TELL YOU WHAT & HOW THE
TIGER <u>THINKS</u>!

HE HATES NOTRE DAME!

1. HE HAS BEEN TOLD OVER & OVER THAT WE PLAY NO
   ONE!
2. HE KNOWS HIS STADIUM <u>NOISE</u> — THE <u>HOSTILE</u>
   CROWD — THE MANIAC EMOTION HE HAS PLAYED WITH
   — WILL RATTLE ANY OPPONENT!
3. HE THINKS NO ONE IS MORE PHYSICALLY <u>TOUGH</u>
   - - - <u>AGILE</u> - - - & IN <u>MENTAL READINESS</u> THAN
   HE IS.
4. HIS <u>COACH</u> IS <u>OBSESSED</u> WITH BEATING NOTRE
   DAME. THAT'S ALL THEY'VE SPOKEN OF. — THE
   PAPERS ARE FULL OF IT. THEY CAN LOSE 4 OR 5
   - - - BUT NOTRE DAME IS THEIR BOWL GAME - - -
   THEIR SEASON.
5. THEIR COACH HAS ALREADY MADE THESE
   STATEMENTS.
   a. "WE WILL WHIP THEM MAN ON MAN, NOTHING
      FANCY."
   b. "WE WILL RUN THEM SIDELINE TO SIDELINE
      - - THEY CANNOT OUT-HIT OR OUT-HUSTLE US."
   c. "NOTRE DAME IS OVERRATED."
6. THEY BELIEVE ALL THIS!

WHEN WE AKE THE FIELD NEARLY 70,000 PEOPLE WILL
HATE <u>YOUR GUTS</u>! A LIVE 300-POUND OR BETTER TIGER
WILL BE MADE TO ROAR THROUGH A MICROPHONE.

THEY WILL PELT YOU WITH FRUIT & CANS. THEY WILL
SWEAR AT YOU. ALL OF THIS GEARED TO CAUSE YOU
- - - "TIMIDITY."

<u>ONE</u> THING WE CAN DEPEND ON - - - - ONE THING WE

MUST HAVE IS A GREAT KNOWLEDGE THAT WE ARE <u>ALL</u> <u>TOGETHER</u> AS A NOTRE DAME TEAM. WE WON'T BREAK! WE WON'T BECOME TIMID, WE WILL NOT BECOME INTIMIDATED. THE 4TH QUARTER OR ANY QUARTER BELONGS TO ANYONE WHO FIGHTS FOR IT.

I HAVE SEEN PLAYERS WHOSE VEINS POPPED OUT — THEIR EYES BULGED — THEY WERE EMOTIONALLY RAVAGING - - - THEY WOULD SCREAM & YELL & GESTURE "YOU DON'T WANT IT - - - & WE DO."

THIS WILL SCARE OFF MANY! THEY WILL STAY CHARGED — YOU CAN BET ON IT. - - - BUT WE ARE NOTRE DAME - - - NEVER FORGET IT!

WHEN THEY PUBLISH "GO TO HELL NOTRE DAME" ON BUMPER STICKERS, I WONDER IF THEY REALLY KNOW WHAT THEY ARE SAYING.

TO WIN THE GAME - - - TO FIGHT VALIANTLY — TO HUSTLE, TO GIVE EVERY OUNCE OF COMPETITIVE CHAMPION YOU CAN MUSTER - - - & DO IT AS A TEAM & THINK <u>WIN</u> - - - ALL THE WAY — IS WHAT WE HAVE GOING FOR US. FOCUS ALL ON WINNING & ON ALL THE THINGS IT TAKES TO WIN.

WE WILL BE BACKED INTO A CORNER - - - BUT WHO SAYS WE CAN'T & WON'T FIGHT OUR WAY OUT. — WE WILL SHOW UP - - - ! GET READY — FOR A HITTING BRAWL, A CONTACT — HUSTLING — NERVE WRACKING AFFAIR - - - & MENTALLY SAY — WE'RE NOT BACKING UP ONE NOTCH - - - WE'VE NEVER QUIT - - - NEVER BROKE - - & HAVE NEVER BEEN INTIMIDATED SO BADLY THAT WE COULDN'T COME BACK.

LASTLY — NOTHING — NO ONE OR NO THINGS — CAN RAISE YOUR EMOTION — TO THE PITCH WE <u>HAVE</u> TO <u>HAVE</u>. JUST <u>YOU</u> & <u>YOUR ACTIONS</u> & YOUR <u>HUSTLE</u> - - & THE WHOLE WEEK'S WORK.

WE ASK EACH OF YOU - - TO GET READY - - - FOR AN EMOTIONAL EXPLOSION FOR THE IRISH. THEY THINK THAT THEY <u>OWN</u> THE PRODUCT.

EACH MAN - - - KNOW WHO YOU PLAY <u>OVER</u> - - - <u>KNOW</u> WHAT YOU MUST DO & GET IT DONE!!!!!

FINAL
The Phantom
NOTRE DAME – 8   LSU – 28

1972

NOTRE DAME VS NORTHWESTERN
9/23/72, GAME #1

"THE PHANTOM SPEAKS"

WHEN, IN YOUR YOUNG LIFETIME, YOU DECIDED TO
COME TO NOTRE DAME; IT INCLUDED MANY REASONS. ALL
OF THEM WERE GOOD AND SOUND! PART OF WHAT THRILLED
YOU WERE THE TALES OF GREAT EFFORT, FANTASTIC
DEDICATION, HIGH TEAM MORALE, AND THE BELIEF THAT
NOTRE DAME ATHLETES WERE MEN SO FULL OF SPIRIT
- - - NOTHING WAS INSURMOUNTABLE.

THE WORLD HAS GROWN MORE SOPHISTICATED NOW.
THERE ARE MANY FINE TEAMS AND COACHES; THERE ARE
MANY MORE CRITICS, MORE ARMCHAIR QUARTERBACKS AND
CAUSTIC INTELLECTUALS THAT WOULD HAVE YOU PLAY AT
ONLY "PASSIVENESS." BUT THINK OF THIS, - - - YOU
ARE NOW NOTRE DAME TO MILLIONS OF PEOPLE.

WHEN WE WERE BEHIND MIAMI FLORIDA BY 1 TOUCHDOWN
LATE IN THE 4TH QUARTER 3 YEARS AGO; WHEN WE HAD
PRACTICED A WEEK IN 6" OF SNOW BEFORE ARRIVING;
WHEN WE WERE HURT WITH INJURIES AND THIS WAS OUR
LAST GAME; WHEN THE HUMIDITY SUCKED EVERY OUNCE OF
ENERGY WE HAD. - - - THAT IS WHEN MIAMI THOUGHT WE
WOULD FOLD! WE WON THE GAME IN THE HEAT — IN THE
HUMIDITY, WITH INJURED PLAYERS REPLACED AND WITH
THEIR OFFICIALS. ONE OF THEIR PLAYERS WAS QUOTED
"POST GAME."

"GOD WHEN THEY BROKE THE HUDDLE ON THAT LAST
DRIVE FOR THE GAME WINNING SCORE, I WAS SPENT
- - - AND I PRACTICE IN THE HEAT - - - BUT THEY
KEPT COMING - - - RUNNING TO THE LINE AND PUNCHING
OUT GAINS - - - IT WAS THEN THAT I KNEW WHY THEY
WERE NOTRE DAME!"

THIS IS, WAS AND WILL ALWAYS BE THE SUPREME
COMPLIMENT. ONE THAT COMES FROM A GUY THAT HAS PAID
THE PRICE AND KNOWS OF WHAT COMPETITIVE GREATNESS
CONSISTS.

WE ARE NOTRE DAME - - - YOU ARE NOTRE DAME.
WE'VE WORKED HARD - - - WE MUST VOW TO NEVER HAVE
A BREAKING POINT! WE MUST RESOLVE THAT
CONDITIONING, MORALE, LEADERSHIP, ENTHUSIASM,

WINNING, BELONG TO THOSE WHO PRACTICE THEM. YOU
BECOME WHAT YOU DO!
   DO GIVE NOTRE DAME A FULL INTERVAL
   IT WILL MAKE US WINNERS - - -
   IT WILL ALLOW US THE RIGHT TO BE
   MEN OF NOTRE DAME - - - IN THE
   BEST SENSE OF THE "PHRASE!"
     BEAT THE WILDCATS!!!

The Phantom

FINAL
NOTRE DAME – 37 NORTHWESTERN – 0

NOTRE DAME VS PURDUE
9/30/72, GAME #2

"THE PHANTOM SPEAKS"

THE NORTHWESTERN APPROACH WAS REALLY A JOY TO BEHOLD. LET ME ENUMERATE A FEW OBSERVATIONS NOT READILY SEEN BY THE AVERAGE FAN.

THERE WAS A "SOUNDNESS" OF PLAY. IT WAS DONE WITH ENTHUSIASTIC EMOTION.

THERE LOOMED NO INDIVIDUALS BUT EACH INDIVIDUAL CARRYING OUT HIS PART. THE JOY FELT FOR THE SUCCESS OF OTHERS WAS SPONTANEOUS!

THERE WAS NO PHONY EMOTION. IT WAS PURE AND NATURAL AND TOTALLY THE PRODUCT OF TEAM AWARENESS — DEDICATION AND HARD WORK - - - <u>NATURAL</u> - - - <u>BEAUTIFUL EMOTION</u>!

HARD WORK - - - YES - - - WE KNEW WHAT WE WERE DOING; WE KNEW IT HAD TO BE DONE TOGETHER! WE KNEW WE WOULD NOT OR COULD NOT BE OUT-CONDITIONED OR OUT-HUSTLED. THEREIN LIES THE JOY!

TWO SEPARATE ENTITIES DEFENSE AND OFFENSE - - - MERGED TO PLAY AND BEAT A COMMON OPPONENT.

TRULY - - - LUCK FOLLOWS PREPARATION. NEVER FORGET THIS - - - A TRUTH IS ALWAYS TRUE. IT WILL BE AGAIN AGAINST PURDUE.

THEY ARE SUPER BIG - - - BUT HAVE LOST TWO CLOSE ONES TO TWO GOOD TEAMS. AND NOW IT BEGINS - - - THE SUPER PSYCH OF OUR OPPONENTS TO "<u>GET NOTRE DAME</u> AND SALVAGE A SEASON!"

PURDUE IS A GOOD FOOTBALL TEAM WHO FIGURES ON SNEAKING UP ON US. DON'T EVER BE LULLED. WHAT PURDUE DOESN'T KNOW AND COULDN'T POSSIBLY SUSPECT IS THAT THIS IS AN OLD TUNE. FOREWARNED IS FORE-ARMED - - - BUT WORDS ALONE WON'T DO IT. WE NEED A REPEAT OF THE GREAT CONSISTENCY OF EXECUTION WE HAD.

WHEN ALL IS SAID AND DONE GREATNESS IN TEAMS OR IN PLAYERS IS NOT A GAME OR A PLAY - - - IT IS IN REPEATED "CONSISTENCY."

GET READY FOR A HEAD KNOCKER, FOR AN EMOTIONAL GAME, FOR ONE THAT WILL TAX US. WE WANT THE WIN

- - - KNOW WHAT MUST BE DONE - - - AND TRULY KNOW
THAT THE REAL FUN IS WINNING. PURDUE-WILL-PLAY-US-
SUPER-CHARGED.
GO GET 'EM IRISH!
BEAT PURDUE!!!

The Phantom

FINAL
NOTRE DAME – 35   PURDUE – 14

NOTRE DAME VS MICHIGAN STATE
10/7/72, GAME #3

"THE PHANTOM SPEAKS"

WHEN YOU PLAN SOMETHING - - - AND YOU WORK AT
IT; I MEAN REALLY WORK AND SWEAT AT IT, AND THEN
SEE IT SUCCEED - - - IT IS AN UNSURPASSED THRILL.

WE PLANNED STRATEGY - - - WE WORKED AT THE
FUNDAMENTALS AND WE SUCCEEDED IN EXECUTING THE
PLAN. WELL DONE! NOT PERFECT - - - SOME ERRORS
- - - SOME FUMBLES, MISSED TACKLES - - - BLOWN
ASSIGNMENTS - - - BUT FEWER THAN THE OPPONENTS.

AS MUCH AS YOU'D LIKE TO SAVOR THE WIN — TO
BASK IN THE WARM GLOW OF VICTORY - - - IT IS A
LUXURY ONLY FOR THE SPECTATOR. PURDUE IS NOW
HISTORY AND ARCH-RIVAL MICHIGAN STATE LOOMS UP.

THEY TOOK A REAL KICKING FROM SOUTHERN CAL
- - - THEY'LL LICK THEIR WOUNDS THOUGH AND FIGHT
YOU IN THEIR BACKYARD - - - THIS YOU CAN BET ON!

WHAT THRILLS ME IS THE GREAT HARMONY OF TEAM
MEMBERS ALL EQUALLY RESOLVED TO DO THEIR OWN JOBS,
ALL SATISFIED IF ONLY WE WIN. THAT IS "TEAMNESS,"
"ONENESS," "SOLIDNESS." A TOUGH, TOUGH FIBER TO
BEND OR BREAK. ONLY THE RUST OF "RIPENESS," OF NOT
RESPECTING THE OPPONENT, OF NOT TREATING EACH GAME
AS THE SINGLY MOST IMPORTANT ONE, ALLOWS THIS KIND
OF FIBER TO FRAY.

MICHIGAN STATE IN EAST LANSING, JUICED UP - - -
RARING TO MAKE THEIR LAST LOSS FORGOTTEN BY
UPSETTING NOTRE DAME, WILL BE A BIG - - - "MUCH
BIGGER" CHALLENGE THAN YOU CAN POSSIBLY KNOW.
EXPECT IT.

WE DON'T HAVE TO BE RAVING EMOTIONAL MANIACS
100% OF THE TIME, BUT WE MUST PREPARE TO MEET A
TEAM READY AND ABLE TO ATTACK US. THERE IS ONLY
ONE MEANS OF PROTECTION; "PREPAREDNESS" - - - WORK
AT THE STRATEGY - - - AT THE EXECUTION. IN YOU
HEART RESOLVE THAT WE'VE GOT A GOOD THING GOING AND
TO KEEP ON GOING ONLY TAKES MORE OF THE SAME.
NEVER IS THERE ROOM FOR A LET UP!

PRESERVE THE ENTHUSIASM, HANG ON TO THE

INTENSITY - - - REMAIN CONSCIENTIOUSLY AWARE OF
"YOUR JOB - - - YOUR PART" AND KEEP ON BUILDING
- - - CLAWING - - - FIGHTING OUR WAY TO THE TOP.
WHEN WE WIN WE RISE! COLORADO - - - TENNESSEE
- - - OTHERS GOT BITTEN - - -. WE NOW KNOW WHAT WE
SUSPECTED - - - WE ARE CAPABLE OF BEING TOP
DRAWER. LET'S NEVER FORGET WHAT CAUSED IT ALL
- - - HARD WORK - - - ENTHUSIASM - - - PRIDE!
LET'S GO GET THE SPARTANS!!!

The Phantom

FINAL
NOTRE DAME – 16   MICHIGAN STATE – 0

NOTRE DAME VS PITTSBURGH
10/14/72, GAME #4

"THE PHANTOM SPEAKS"

PLAUDITS TO THE DEFENSE - - - FINE EFFORT, GREAT
SHUTOUT!

OFFENSE - - - WE WERE NOT ASSIGNMENT-COMPETENT!
WE DID NOT KNOCK PEOPLE DOWN! WE FUMBLED - - - WE
RAN WRONG ROUTES AND MISSED ASSIGNMENTS - - - ALL
OF THIS IN A PRESSURE GAME AND WE WERE LUCKY TO
WIN THROUGH STELLAR DEFENSE AND THE KICKING GAME
. . . <u>BUT</u> WE WON. NEVER FORGET THAT THIS IS THE
ULTIMATE OBJECTIVE.

MAYBE WE GREW UP A LITTLE - - - MAYBE THE
PRESSURE OF A TIGHT BALL GAME SHOWED US EARLY THAT
<u>EVERY</u> OPPONENT DEMANDS YOUR BEST EFFORT, YOUR BEST
CONCENTRATION, YOUR BEST PREPARATION.

NORTHWESTERN, PURDUE, MICHIGAN STATE ARE ALL
HISTORY. WE MUST CONCENTRATE ON THE NEXT OPPONENT
- - - THE ONLY OPPONENT, THE ONE WE PLAY NEXT
- - - PITTSBURGH.

PHYSICALLY THEY ARE BIG - - - THEY HAVE A POOR
RECORD - - - THEY WILL RALLY AS ALL <u>UNDERDOGS DO</u>,
TO SHOW YOU. NEVER - - - EVER - - - TAKE ANYTHING
FOR GRANTED - - - YOU MUST ALWAYS PAY A PRICE TO
WIN WELL.

WHEN A TEAM WHO HAS NOTHING TO LOSE - - - NO
SHAME - - - OR FACE TO SAVE - - - THEY WILL SELL
OUT AGAINST YOU. THIS IS THE PRICE THE VICTOR PAYS
AND IT IS SMALL WHEN COMPARED TO LOSING.

THE IDEA OF A GREAT TEAM IS SELFLESSNESS,
HARMONY - - - GREAT ENTHUSIASM WEEKLY RENEWED. IT
IS "SOUNDNESS," "VERVE," "SUPER EFFORT." WE WERE
"LUKEWARM" AGAINST OUR LAST OPPONENT. WE DIDN'T PAY
THEM PROPER RESPECT.

WE BEAT A PRETTY FAIR FOOTBALL TEAM AND ONE THAT
PLAYED VERY WELL AGAINST US.

PITTSBURGH - - - THE BIG TEAM, THE WINLESS TEAM
- - - DO WE DARE LOOK DOWN OUR NOSE AT THEM? - - -
NOT AS LONG AS FOOTBALL IS PLAYED! ANY ELEVEN MEN
CAN BEAT ANY ELEVEN MEN, ANYTIME, ANYWHERE - - -.

HOW CAN A YOUNG PLAYER LEARN THIS - - - WITHOUT
SUFFERING THE SCAR OF EXPERIENCE? THE ONLY WAY WE
KNOW IS FOR YOU TO BELIEVE HISTORY - - - IT ALWAYS
PROVES SO!

NO PLAYER IS SO BLESSED TO PRACTICE POORLY
- - - OR PLAY POORLY - - - AND NOT SUFFER, AND IN
TURN CAUSE OUR TEAM TO SUFFER. DON'T YOU PERSONALLY
LET IT HAPPEN TO _YOU_!

WORK - - - GET EXCITED - - - KNOW YOU JOB AND
THE EXECUTION.

PERFORMANCE COUNTS - - - NOT POTENTIAL - - -
NOT ALIBIS - - - NOT ANYTHING BUT THE JOB YOU'VE
GOT TO DO! HOW DO YOU BECOME A CHAMPION? YOU
PERFORM!

GO IRISH!! BEAT THE PANTHERS!!!

The Phantom

FINAL
NOTRE DAME – 42   PITTSBURGH – 16

A PHANTOM SPECIAL
(AFTER — PITT)

FOLLOW THIS ILLOGICAL "LOGIC."

NOTRE DAME AT THE SEASON'S OPEN IS "<u>GREEN</u>" AND "YOUNG." NO ONE EXPECTS MUCH!

WE WIN - - - WE'RE ENTHUSED AND HAPPY! WE BEAT PURDUE BIG AND THEY WERE HIGHLY THOUGHT OF. WE WERE STILL EXCITED.

WE PLAY MICHIGAN STATE AFTER THEY TOOK A SHELLACKING FROM SOUTHERN CAL - - - WHICH MICHIGAN STATE CONTRIBUTED TO HEAVILY.

NOW THE <u>ILLOGIC</u> BEGINS TO SET IN. WHAT'S WRONG WITH THE SUPER TEAM? WHAT'S WRONG WITH THE IRISH? "HELL, DON'T THEY HAVE ALL THAT SUPER TALENT - - - SHOULDN'T THEY ROLL OVER EVERYONE?"

<u>UNKNOWING</u> - - - WRITERS AND SPECTATORS AND PROFESSORS - - - AND FANS HAVE COME TO <u>EXPECT</u> EASY WINS.

THEY NEVER CREDIT THE OPPONENT. THIS SEEPS INTO THE TEAM. THE TEAM WINS 16-0 AND FEELS BADLY.

WE PLAY PITT - - - THEY'VE BEEN LOSERS - - - WE CRACK THEM LATE FOR A 42-16 WIN. YOU WOULD THINK "HURRAY" "SUPER" "GREAT" - - - "WE'RE 4 & 0." ANYWHERE ELSE AT ANYTIME YES - - - BUT THE SEEPING OF THE "OUTSIDE" TAKES AWAY OUR JOY - - - ROBS US OF SAVORING THE WIN.

WE ENTER THE LOCKER ROOM <u>SORRY</u> - - - APOLOGETICALLY - - - WE DIDN'T MAKE THEM LOOK LIKE KINDERGARTEN KIDS. NOW HEAR THIS! THE COACHES ARE <u>AWARE</u> OF THE "YOU DIDN'T LOOK GOOD WINNING SYNDROME."

THE COACHES SAY TO HELL WITH THAT - - - "WE WON." LET'S NEVER LOSE SIGHT OF THAT. LET'S BE SMART ENOUGH TO BE JOYOUS AND CELEBRATE AND GIVE THANKS FOR VICTORY, AT LEAST IN THOSE MOMENTS WHERE WE CAN.

NO MATTER WHAT THE CIRCUMSTANCES, NO MATTER WHO PLAYED WELL OR POORLY, COLLECTIVELY WE DID WHAT WE SET OUT TO DO - - — - - WE WON!

WE WON ALL THE WAY TO SUNDAY NIGHT WHEN WE

CORRECT MISTAKES. WHETHER BY ONE POINT OR 100
- - - WE WON! THAT IS ENOUGH.

LET US NOT BECOME VICTIMS OF A <u>SYNDROME</u> IMPOSED
ON US BY OUTSIDERS. OUR OPPONENTS ARE WORTHY AND
THEY DON'T THINK BEATING THEM WILL BE EASY - - -
WHY DO WE?

CONGRATULATIONS - - - WE'RE A GOOD TEAM. LET'S
STAY A HAPPY TEAM - - - AND NEVER <u>LOOK BACK</u>.

LET NO ONE <u>SUBTRACT</u> FROM THE VICTORY - - - -

The Phantom

NOTRE DAME VS MISSOURI
10/21/72, GAME #5

"THE PHANTOM SPEAKS"

A GREAT LEADER ONCE ASKED OF HIS COLLEAGUES AND
ADVISORS - - - "SINCE I PROVIDE FOR YOU, CLOTHE
YOU, AND RULE YOU, I ASK FOR THE PAYMENT OF ONE
GREAT "TRUTH."

MANY TRIED TO CONVEY A TRUTH BUT ONLY TRIVIAL
AND MEANINGLESS ITEMS THAT WERE CONTEMPORARY IDEAS
WERE OFFERED. THE OLDEST AND MOST HUMBLE OF THE
CROWD, CLOSED-MOUTHED UNTIL NOW - - - SPOKE. "I
KNOW ONLY ONE GREAT TRUTH - - - IT IS, "AND THIS
TOO SHALL PASS!"

WHAT DOES THIS MEAN IN REGARDS TO YOU THE NOTRE
DAME TEAM OR SPECIFICALLY YOU THE NOTRE DAME
PLAYERS?

WHAT IS FUN? AND WHAT IS SORROW? AND WHAT IS
WORK AND WHAT IS PLAY? IT WILL ALL BE OVER AND
DONE & PASSED IN 6 SHORT WEEKS. THAT IS A TRUTH!
YOU CANNOT RECAPTURE IT, BACK IT UP AND REPLAY IT
- - -, BUT ONLY DO IT ONCE.

LIFE IS LIKE TOOTHPASTE - - - WHEN YOU SQUEEZE
IT OUT OF THE TUBE, YOU CANNOT PUT IT BACK IN. WE
HAVE WON 4 GAMES - - - WE HAVE 6 TO PLAY. WE
CANNOT EVER PLAY THEM OUT OF NUMERICAL ORDER. #5
IS THE NEXT GAME AND OPPONENT. IT IS MISSOURI.

EVERY WEEK THE NEXT OPPONENT IS THE MOST
IMPORTANT GAME TO BE PLAYED.

THE MORE WE WIN, THE MORE THE OPPONENT GETS
PSYCHED TO BEAT US. THERE CAN BE NO EASY WINS NOW.
THE VICTORIES THAT SHOULD COME, SHOULD BE BECAUSE
OF BETTER PREPARATION - - - FEWER MISTAKES AND A
GREAT AWARENESS THAT WHEN IT IS OVER IT IS ALL
OVER!

FOR THE REST OF YOUR LIVES AFTER YOUR PLAYING
DAYS ARE GONE, YOU'LL WISH AND PRAY AND HOPE TO
RECAPTURE OR RE-PLAY JUST ONE GAME. IT CAN NEVER
HAPPEN. ANYTHING YOU HOPE TO ACHIEVE OR DO MUST BE
DONE NOW!

I TOO KNOW A TRUTH: "ENERGY FOLLOWS THOUGHT"

- - - PITTSBURGH HAD ENERGY TO WIN UNTIL THEY
THOUGHT THEY COULDN'T (ENTER DREW MAHALIC'S TIMELY
INTERCEPTION"). THEY THEN WERE A DIFFERENT TEAM.
THAT WAS THEIR BREAKING POINT.

ALL THOUGHT PROVOKES DIRECTION AND ENERGY.
IMAGINE THE MAGNITUDE OF AN ENTIRE TEAM WITH BUT
ONE THOUGHT. THOUGHT IS DESIRE AND PRAYER AND
EFFORT AND DEDICATION AND LOYALTY. IT EXPLODES INTO
ENERGY AND ACTION. THIS ONE CONCEPT IS WHY "NO ARMY
IS AS POWERFUL AS AN IDEA WHOSE TIME HAS COME! DO
YOU HEAR? NO ARMY OR MISSOURI OR ANYONE — ! GET AN
IDEA - - - GO TO WORK. BE SOUND - - - BE WITH IT!
BEAT MISSOURI!!!

The Phantom

FINAL
NOTRE DAME – 26   MISSOURI – 30

NOTRE DAME VS TCU
10/28/72, GAME #6

"THE PHANTOM SPEAKS"

WHEN WE WIN - - - WE CANNOT ENJOY IT FOR LONGER
THAN A DAY. THE SAME REASON INSISTS THAT <u>THIS MUST
ALSO BE TRUE OF A LOSS</u>. LOSING HURTS - - - IT
STINKS - - - IT IS THE WORST THING THAT CAN HAPPEN
TO A TEAM, BUT TO LIVE WITH IT LONGER THAN WE
SHOULD IS A MISTAKE. MISSOURI DIDN'T LIVE WITH
THEIR NEBRASKA LOSS FOR LONG - - - THEY REGROUPED
AND REDEDICATED.

ERRORS HURT US - - - WE MUST CORRECT THOSE IN
THE FUTURE. THERE IS ONLY THE <u>FUTURE</u>, FOR NOTHING
IN THE PAST COUNTS - - -; IT IS HISTORY!

IN PEOPLE - - - THERE ARE 3 DISTINCT BREAKDOWNS:

1. YESTERDAY PEOPLE - - - TIED TO HISTORY,
   NOSTALGIC "WHEN I WAS YOUNG" AND "WAY BACK
   WHEN" TYPES OF MEMORIES.
2, TODAY PEOPLE - - - NOT CARING OF WHAT WENT
   BEFORE OR WHAT COMES AFTER - - - "EAT, DRINK
   & BE MERRY - - - NOW!"
3. TOMORROW PEOPLE - - - RESPECTFUL OF THE PAST
   - - - AWARE OF TODAY - - - PLANNING FOR
   TOMORROW - - - <u>THAT</u> IS THE ROUTE WE MUST
   TAKE.

<u>RESPECTFUL</u> ABOUT WHAT HAS PRECEDED US TO ALWAYS
ALLOW US TO BE THE TEAM PEOPLE GET UP FOR - - -

<u>AWARE</u> - - - THAT WE BEAT OURSELVES THROUGH
ERRORS.

<u>PLANNING</u> - - - TO BOUNCE BACK LIKE CHAMPIONS
- - - WE NEVER QUIT TRYING. THAT'S THE THRILL THE
CHALLENGE AND REWARD!

TEXAS CHRISTIAN IS 5 & 1. THEY ARE BIG AND A
GOOD SOUND FOOTBALL TEAM.

WE'VE GOT TO GET BACK ON THE WINNING TRACK.
WE'VE GOT TO OVERCOME ADVERSITY TOGETHER - - - JUST
AS WE SHARED THE <u>GOOD</u> TOGETHER.

NO ONE PLACES BLAME NOR SHOULD ANYONE BE THE
SOLE RECIPIENT. IF <u>WE REALLY ARE</u> A TEAM, WE SHOULD
COLLECTIVELY LOSE, BECAUSE WE DID. WE CAN ALSO

REDEDICATE - - - REGROUP - - - BOUNCE BACK - - -
AND COLLECTIVELY GET OFF THE SEAT OF OUR PANTS FROM
A 9 COUNT - - - AND HAMMER OUT A WIN.

IT WON'T BE EASY! THERE ARE TWO TIMES WHEN IT
IS MOST DIFFICULT TO WIN. (1) WHEN YOU EXPECT TO
- - - (2) WHEN YOU HAVE JUST LOST.

ADVERSITY WHEN COMBINED WITH CHARACTER - - -
GIVES RISE TO EXCELLENCE. THAT'S WHAT WE'RE AFTER!

BEAT TEXAS CHRISTIAN - - - "<u>AND NEVER BREATHE A
WORD ABOUT YOUR LOSS</u>."

The Phantom

FINAL
NOTRE DAME – 21   TCU – 0

NOTRE DAME VS NAVY
11/4/72, GAME #7

"THE PHANTOM SPEAKS"

WHEN WE WIN - - - THE WORLD IS RIGHT! WE BEAT A
FINE FOOTBALL TEAM - - - OUR <u>DEFENSE</u> PLAYED SUPER!
THEY DESERVE ACCOLADES AND DESERVED THE SHUTOUT.

IS IT ANY QUESTION TO ANYONE THAT DEFENSE IS
DESIRE, IT IS PRIDE, IT IS BEING INCENSED WITH
EMOTION? THOSE THREE THINGS DESCRIBED THE SWARMING,
THE GANG-TACKLING, THE HIGH EMOTION THE DEFENSE
<u>FELT</u>. TRULY THESE ARE THE QUALITIES OF NOTRE DAME'S
GREAT DEFENSIVE TEAMS. TO REPEAT THEM WE MUST BE
AWARE THAT THEY DO NOT REGENERATE THEMSELVES. THE
TEAM AND ESPECIALLY INDIVIDUAL PLAYERS AND COACHES
- - - MUST DO IT FOR EACH NEW OPPONENT.

OFFENSE: WE MOVED THE BALL - - - BUT COULD HAVE
BROKEN THE GAME SOONER HAD WE NOT <u>FUMBLED</u>. A FUMBLE
IS THE WORST THING A PLAYER CAN DO TO THE REST OF
HIS TEAM. IT IS EQUAL TO MINUS <u>40</u> YARDS. THE
AVERAGE OF A PUNT! WHY DO PEOPLE FUMBLE?

1. ARM TOO FAR AWAY FROM BODY.
2. FINGERS NOT WEBBED OVER THE END OF BALL.
3. WRONG ARM CARRY.
4. ON CONTACT - - - NOT AWARE OF BALL.
5. LACK OF TOTAL CONCENTRATION.
6, ACCIDENT OR GREAT HIT BY DEFENDER.

EXAMINE THESE IF YOU ARE ENTRUSTED WITH THE
BALL. WORK ON THESE THINGS DAILY. LET US IMPROVE
THIS PART OF OUR GAME.

AND NOW NAVY - - - AN IMPROVED FOOTBALL TEAM.
THEY HAVE BEATEN AIR FORCE. THEY ARE <u>QUICK</u>, SUPER-
DISCIPLINED PLAYERS. THEY WILL NOT BREAK EASILY.

WE MUST POUR OVER THEM AGAIN, MATCHING THEIR
INTENSITY, AND INTENSE THEY WILL BE. "PLAY WELL
AGAINST NOTRE DAME AND GET YOURSELF A REPUTATION."

NAVY WILL BE TOUGH - - - <u>UNLESS</u> WE HAVE LEARNED
THAT WHEN ALL ELSE IS EQUAL - - - EMOTION IS THE
NAME OF THE GAME. IT IS THE DIVIDER BETWEEN <u>WINNER</u>
AND <u>LOSER</u>.

IT ASKS OF THE CONTESTANTS: <u>WHO WANTS — WHO</u>

DESIRES — WHO FEELS — WHO WILL PAY THE PRICE?

IT ANSWERS: THE VICTOR WANTS IT THE MOST! THIS THEN, IS THE EDGE - - - NOT BRAWN — NOT STRATEGY — NOT PAPERWORK!

IF WE WANT TO WIN - - - WE SURELY KNOW WHAT IT COSTS. LET US GO ON THEM ARMED WITH PAST KNOWLEDGE AND FUTURE EXPECTATIONS OF WHAT WE MUST DO TO WIN - - - TO BEAT NAVY - - - "NO — LOSING!"

The Phantom

FINAL
NOTRE DAME – 42   NAVY – 23

NOTRE DAME VS AIR FORCE
11/11/72, GAME #8

"THE PHANTOM SPEAKS"

OFFENSE PLAYED WELL - - - DEFENSE PLAYED SPOTTY
BUT THE TOTAL OUTCOME IS A WIN 42-23 OVER NAVY. IT
IS VERY IMPORTANT TO REMEMBER THAT WE ARE NOT TWO
TEAMS BUT TWO COMPONENTS OF THE SAME TEAM WITH BUT
ONE GOAL; TO WIN!

ON CERTAIN PLAYS OR CERTAIN DAYS ONE PHASE HAS A
BETTER OR EASIER TIME OF THINGS. WE ARE A TOTAL
TEAM, HOWEVER, AND THE OFFENSE OR DEFENSE DOESN'T
LOSE OR WIN - - - NOTRE DAME DOES. IT IS OUR 6th
WIN AND THOUGH IT WAS NOT AS WE WOULD HAVE LIKED,
IT GOES INTO THE RECORD AS A WIN OVER NAVY.

THE OBJECT NOW IS TO GATHER UP THE MISTAKES
- - - CORRECT THEM - - - AND GO ON TO BEAT AIR
FORCE.

SERVICE TEAM - - - QUICK - - - STICKY - - -
SPIRITED - - - MUCH EMOTION - - - UPSET BENT ON
THEIR HOME FIELD. THE OPPONENT, OR IN THE LAST TWO
CASES, NAVY AND NOW AIR FORCE, HAVE NO PREMIUM OR
LOCK ON "EMOTION." THE IRISH HAVE SOME "PRIDE AND
EMOTION" TOO.

A LOOK BACK TO THE LAST TIME WE PLAYED AIR
FORCE OUT THERE IN COLORADO SPRINGS. THEY MARCHED
SEVERAL THOUSAND STRONG TO GREET US - - - THEY
ROARED THEIR CHEERS INTO A MICROPHONE, THEY SHOT
OFF A CANNON WHEN THEY WENT AHEAD OF THE IRISH 7
TO 0. THEY WERE SUPER-CHARGED - - - THEY FELT NAVY
AND ARMY WERE NOT IN THEIR CLASS. THEY LOST ONLY
THOSE TWO, NOT BEING EMOTIONAL. THEY'LL BE READY
FOR US. THIS IS THE AIR FORCE BOWL GAME.

WE ARE A SOUND TEAM, WITH SOME INJURIES - - -
BUT SOME YOUNG PEOPLE FILLING IN. WORK AT THIS, GET
READY, PREPARE - - - BE THOROUGH AND CONSCIENTIOUS
AND <u>BE HITTERS</u>. NOW YOU KNOW THE MAKEUP OF SERVICE
TEAMS - - - THEY SPEAR, THEY PILE - - - THEY ARE
EXCELLENTLY CONDITIONED AND <u>THEY NEVER SAY</u> "UNCLE."

WE MUST NEVER GIVE THEM A REASON TO THINK THEY
CAN DO IT TO US. WE MUST ATTACK AND KEEP PUNCHING

FOR A FULL 60 MINUTES WITH <u>DEFENSE</u>, WITH <u>OFFENSE</u>, WITH <u>KICKING</u> GAME, AND WE CAN OWN A GREAT VICTORY AND JOYOUS RIDE HOME - - - - - - - - - - GET READY FOR OUR 8th GAME — OUR 7th WIN AND A HITTING CONTEST!!

BEAT THE AIR FORCE!!!!!!

The Phantom

FINAL
NOTRE DAME – 21   AIR FORCE – 7

NOTRE DAME VS MIAMI (FLA)
11/18/72, GAME #9

"THE PHANTOM SPEAKS"

AIR FORCE IS <u>OVER</u>! WE WON IT AND WE ARE SEVEN
AND ONE. THAT'S BEAUTIFUL, AND THEY CAN SAY
ANYTHING THEY WANT, WE <u>BEAT</u> THEM AND IT'S OVER!
WHEN ALL IS SAID AND DONE, THE SCOREBOARD IS FINAL
JUDGE. THEY TRIED TO STEAL IT FROM US, BUT WE
NEVER BROKE!

AND NOW WHAT? - - - MIAMI WHO LOOKED PAST
TAMPA! MIAMI, SHOOTING FOR NOTRE DAME! MIAMI - - -
RECRUITING ANY POOR STUDENT, AND ANYTHING GOES TO
GET THE RECRUIT! MIAMI - - - GONNA MAKE A
REPUTATION ON NOTRE DAME!

SO WHAT ELSE IS NEW? DOESN'T EVERYONE GET "UP"
FOR US? DOESN'T EVERYONE PREACH "UPSET" NOTRE DAME?

NOW LET US SAY IT LIKE IT IS. IT IS TOUGH
ENOUGH TO MATCH EACH NEW OPPONENT'S EMOTION,
BECAUSE WHAT IS "<u>*THE* GAME</u>" FOR THEM IS JUST "<u>THE
NEXT GAME</u>" TO US. YOU HAVE GOT TO KNOW THAT MIAMI
LOOKED RIGHT PAST TAMPA! NOW THEY WILL COME HERE
TRYING TO AVENGE THEIR LOST PRIDE.

WHAT IS TOUGHER - - - THEY ARE A DAMNED GOOD
FOOTBALL TEAM! THEIR OFFENSIVE BACKFIELD IS THE
BIGGEST AND FASTEST WE'VE MET. THEIR MIDDLE GUARD,
#70, IS CHRISTIANI AND THE QUICKEST MIDDLE GUARD
WE'LL MEET. HE IS THE YOUNG MAN WHO INJURED BILL
ETTER'S KNEE A YEAR AGO. IT WAS NOT INTENTIONAL,
BUT AFTER THAT PLAY - - - HE PARADED AFTER EVERY
TACKLE - - - HIS ARMS THROWN UP WITH DOUBLE
CLENCHED FISTS IN AN ATTITUDE OF "IT WAS ME - - -
I DID IT." THEY WILL BE VERY PSYCHED, AND THEY
WILL DO THEIR DAMNEDEST TO UPSET US. WE HAVE COME
A LONG HARD WAY - - - TOO LONG AND TOO HARD TO LET
UP. THIS IS THE LAST TIME MEN LIKE <u>MARX</u>
- - - <u>MUSURACA</u> - - - <u>SCHLEZES</u> - - - <u>O'MALLEY</u> WILL
EVER PLAY ON NOTRE DAME TURF FOR THE DEFENSE. (PLUS
A HOST OF OTHER SENIORS).

<u>DAMPEER</u> - - - <u>CREANEY</u> - - - <u>DREW</u> - - - <u>HUFF</u>
- - - <u>CISCO</u> - - - <u>DEWAN</u> - - - THIS IS YOUR FINALE

IN OUR STADIUM. WE WANT A GOOD MEMORY - - - WE
WANT AN "UP" - - - EMOTIONAL, GOOD, FUN TIME. WE
OWE OURSELVES A SALUTE BEFORE WE GO ON FOR OUR
10TH GAME. LET'S GET READY FOR A "KNOCKING AFFAIR"
- - - LET'S PUT OUR HEARTS INTO THE LAST HOME GAME
- - - AND FOR OUR SENIORS - - - A FAREWELL THAT
LEAVES US FULL OF <u>PRIDE</u>.

MIAMI - - - WILL BE SHOCKED TO KNOW THEY ARE
NOT SNEAKING UP ON US! THAT'S THE WAY IT SHOULD
BE. GET IT DONE. <u>BEAT MIAMI</u>!!!

The Phantom

FINAL
NOTRE DAME – 20   MIAMI (FLA) – 17

NOTRE DAME VS USC
12/2/72, GAME #10

"THE PHANTOM SPEAKS"

SO FEW MOMENTS IN LIFE GIVE YOU A CHANCE TO
PLAN FOR THEM . . . YET WE HAVE SUCH AN
OPPORTUNITY! WE PLAY THE "<u>SUPERTEAM</u>" - - - AT LEAST
THAT IS WHAT THEY'VE BEEN TABBED. I SEE IT
DIFFERENTLY - - - LIFE HAS TAUGHT ME MORE THAN
ONCE THAT NOTHING IS PREDETERMINED - - - THERE IS
NOT CERTAINTY - - - NOTHING IS A SURE THING!

ALL OF THIS FAVORS THE IRISH FORTUNE! RIGHT NOW
THE COLLEGE FOOTBALL WORLD DOESN'T GIVE US A
"SNOWBALL'S CHANCE IN HELL." THEY OVERLOOK A FEW
THINGS. SOUTHERN CAL MUST FIELD A TEAM - - - THE
SAME NUMBER AS WE DO. THEY MUST <u>BLOCK</u>, TACKLE AND
CLAW THEIR WAY TO WIN - - - BECAUSE THAT'S WHAT
WINNING IS ALL ABOUT - - - IT TAKES EFFORT.

FORTUNE - - - FAVORS THE BOLD! BE BOLD ENOUGH
TO BELIEVE IN YOURSELVES. HAVE CRUST ENOUGH TO
MENTALLY CONCEIVE THAT <u>WE CAN</u> BEAT <u>THEM</u>.

THERE HAVE BEEN MOMENTS IN COMPETITION WHERE MY
LEGS TREMBLED AND MY TEETH SHOOK, BUT MY HEART AND
HEAD WERE SOLID - - - AND IN SO BELIEVING IN
MYSELF - - - GREAT THINGS HAPPENED. ALL ODDS CAN
BE OVERCOME.

I FIRMLY BELIEVE IN THIS PHILOSOPHY AS A WAY OF
LIFE. NO ONE CAN BE BEATEN IF <u>THEY ABSOLUTELY</u>
<u>REFUSE TO BE</u>!

THAT IS THE SECRET - - - WE WILL NOT BREAK!
BELIEVE ME WHEN I TELL YOU THAT THEY ARE PLANNING
THE SUPREME "SLAP IN THE FACE."

THEY FIGURE THEIR GREAT DEPTH AND SIZE AND SPEED
WILL RUN THROUGH US LIKE A BB THROUGH PAPER. ALL
OF THE STAGE IS SET THE WAY IT MUST BE.

NO ONE GIVES US A CHANCE BUT OURSELVES. WE CAN
BLOCK - - - WE CAN RUN - - - WE CAN TACKLE. WE ARE
CAPABLE OF GREAT EMOTION, WE HAVE SPIRIT - - -
COHESIVENESS — LEADERSHIP - - - DESIRE AND MUCH
<u>PRIDE</u>. WHAT ELSE DOES IT TAKE - - -? JUST ONE
THING - - - THE <u>ACTION</u> OF DOING IT. WORDS AND

PHRASES - - - ARE EMPTY - - - THEY MEAN LITTLE;
ACTIONS COUNT!

SET YOURSELF - - - THINK ABOUT HITTING AND
SUSTAINING A GREAT INTERVAL. THINK ABOUT NO
BREAKING POINT. THINK ABOUT "PRIDE" - - - AND NOTRE
DAME'S GREAT OPPORTUNITY. THE ENTIRE TV SCENE
EXPECTS TO SEE YOUR DEMISE. THEY NEVER LOOKED INTO
OUR HEARTS!!

I REMEMBER SOUTHERN CAL EXPLODING ON OUR FIELD
INTO A FIGHT THROUGH ANGER - - - AND EMOTION. TWO
CAN PLAY AT THAT.

I REMEMBER THEM OUT THERE TRYING FOR A ROMP WITH
4 TOUCHDOWNS IN THE LEAD.

I RECALL OUR SQUAD HUDDLING ON THE SIDELINE AND
SAYING TO EACH OTHER, "BABIES - - - ONE THING
WE'RE NOT IS QUITTERS - - - HERE WE COME YOU SONS
OF - - —. AND WE DID!"

"OKAY" - - - "TROJANS" - - -"GIANTS" - - - "BIG
BAD GUYS." HANG ONTO YOUR FANNIES BECAUSE IF WE ARE
OF ONE MIND TO DO IT - - - IT'LL GET DONE.

I'M PICKING THE IRISH - - - NOT ON SENTIMENT
- - - BUT ON HEART. LET'S GET THE JOB DONE AND
UPSET SOUTHERN CAL! LET'S BELIEVE IN US!

BEAT THE TROJANS!!!!!!!!!!!!

The Phantom

FINAL
NOTRE DAME – 23   USC – 45

1973

NOTRE DAME VS NORTHWESTERN
9/22/73, GAME #1

"THE PHANTOM SPEAKS"

MANY TIMES AND MANY PEOPLE SAY NOTRE DAME WINS
FOR SOME OR ALL OF THE FOLLOWING REASONS:
1. SHE GETS ALL THE SUPER TALENT THAT THE
   CATHOLIC NUNS AND PRIESTS SEND HER.
2. SHE PSYCHS MOST OPPONENTS BY HER MYTHICAL
   TRADITION.
3. SHE NEVER RECRUITS - - - THEY JUST ALL WANT
   TO GO THERE.
   a. WE OF NOTRE DAME KNOW THE TRUTH! OUR SUPER
      TALENT IS ONLY IN <u>BELIEVING IN OURSELVES,
      PREPARING AND PERFORMING</u>. NO ONE HAS SUPER
      TALENT.
   b. WE PSYCH NOBODY — THEY ARE ALL UP IN THE
      "BIT" TO PLAY US - - - TO "GET A REPUTA-
      TION" OR "MAKE THEIR SEASON." <u>WE HAVE NEVER
      PLAYED</u> A FLAT <u>OPPONENT</u>.
   c. NOT EVERYONE GOES HERE, ONLY PLAYERS WHO
      SAW THROUGH THE GLITTER OF "EXTRA" OFFERS
      AND RECRUITING GUISES. NOTRE DAME PLAYERS
      WERE DIFFERENT BY CHOICE. THEY WILL PLAY
      DIFFERENT - - - BY CHOICE.
THEY CHOOSE TO HOLD VERY SACRED, A PRINCIPLE OF
COMPETITION. IT IS AS FOLLOWS - - - AND I EXPLAIN
IT FOR THE YOUNGER PLAYERS. "WE NEVER HAVE A
BREAKING POINT."
A BREAKING POINT IN LIFE, IN COMPETITION, IN AN
ARGUMENT, IN ANY KIND OF STRUGGLE - - - IS WHERE
ONE OR THE OTHER COMPETITORS "BREAK." THEY GIVE UP
- - - THEY SAY, IN EFFECT, "UNCLE" - - - "I'VE HAD
IT" - - - "WE'RE TOO FAR BEHIND." "IT CAN'T BE
DONE." ALL LOSING OPPONENTS, WHETHER IN THE FIRST
OR LAST MINUTE OR SOMEWHERE IN BETWEEN, MENTALLY
SAY THIS FACT.
THIS IDEA PRECEDES THE ACTION!
OUR IDEA IS WE NEVER SAY IT. "WHAT THO THE
ODDS" - - - WHATEVER BAD BREAK - - - WHATEVER THE
SITUATION - - - WE WON'T BREAK! THAT IS OUR <u>OPEN</u>

SECRET. THAT IS WHY WE ARE NOTRE DAME. <u>WE ALL</u> ARE
A PART OF THIS PHILOSOPHY - - - POSITIVE THOUGHT
PLUS POSITIVE ACTIONS END IN POSITIVE RESULTS.
                    BEAT NORTHWESTERN!!!!!!

The Phantom

FINAL
NOTRE DAME – 44   NORTHWESTERN – 0

NOTRE DAME VS PURDUE
9/29/73, GAME #2

"THE PHANTOM SPEAKS"

WELL DONE! BUT NEVER LOOK FOR PRAISE BEFORE IT
IS DUE. IT IS DUE WITH A COMPLETED TASK. OUR TASK
WAS LAST SATURDAY 10% OF OUR OVERALL GOAL. IF YOU
SEEK MORE OF PRAISE AND LESS OF "PERFECTION" YOU
BECOME — FAT AND HAPPY - - - "SATISFIED." BUT THE
GAUNT — HUNGRY — COMPETITOR CAN NEVER FEED HIS
"PRIDE IN ACCOMPLISHMENT" QUITE ENOUGH. AN INNER
WISDOM TELLS HIM, "WHOA-BABY - - - THAT'S ONE GAME
AND IT IS OVER - - - IT MEANS NOTHING!" WE WILL
SNEAK UP ON NO ONE. WE WILL PLAY NO ONE NOT
PSYCHED TO THE SKY. NORTHWESTERN IS HISTORY.

WE ALL APPRECIATE "GREATNESS" IN PLAYERS, A
TEAM, OR A COACH. THIS "GREATNESS" IS HIGH LEVEL
PERFORMANCE REPEATED OVER AND OVER WITH HIGH
CONSISTENCY - - - NOT JUST FLASHES HERE AND THERE.
WE SHOWED A FLASH, BUT WHO REALLY KNOWS HOW GOOD
THEY WERE OR HOW GOOD WE ARE? TIME WILL TELL HOW
CONSISTENTLY WE PERFORM. TAKE ALL OF THE X'S - - -
KEEP ALL OF O'S, SCRAP THE UNIFORMS - - - THE
BANDS - - - THE WRITERS AND CATCH PHRASES OF
PRAISE - - - I'LL TAKE IN PLACE OF THEM A GREAT
DESIRE TO WIN, WILD ENTHUSIASTIC GROUP PLAYING AS
"ONE." ONE MIND, ONE GOAL, ONE SOLIDIFIED EFFORT.
LET US NEVER BE A VICTIM OF THIS STRENGTH - - -
BUT LET IT ALWAYS BE OUR ARMOR. WE WILL HAVE TO BE
"ONE" VERSUS PURDUE. REMEMBERING FOOTBALL IS A TEAM
GAME. ONLY THE BEST TEAM WINS. AVERAGE PLAYERS
SUPERIOR IN TEAM PLAY, CAN BEAT GREAT INDIVIDUAL
ATHLETES IF THEY PLAY SEPARATE WAYS. UNITY IS
STRENGTH.

IF A BAND OF FIGHTING IRISH IS OF ONE MIND,
WITH GREAT EFFORT — GREAT EXECUTION, GREAT
ENDURANCE - - - IF THEY PLAY WITH WILD ENTHUSIASM
AND "NO BREAKING POINT" - - - WE WILL WIN!
POSITIVE RESULTS COME FROM POSITIVE THOUGHTS - - -
WORK - - - AND DEEDS! LET US TOGETHER PLAN - - -

PRAY AND PLAY WITH <u>CLASS</u>, WITH POISE - - - AND
<u>SPIRIT</u>.

WHEN ALL THINGS ARE EQUAL - - - THIS IS THE
BIGGEST EDGE OF ALL! AND IS BROUGHT ABOUT BY YOU
- - - VOWING TO DO YOUR PART. WE WILL BE AS STRONG
AS OUR WEAKEST PLAYER. SAY TO YOURSELF - - - "IT
WILL NEVER BE ME" AND WORK TO THAT END!

The Phantom

FINAL
NOTRE DAME – 20   PURDUE 7

NOTRE DAME VS MICHIGAN STATE
10/6/73, GAME #3

"THE PHANTOM SPEAKS"

TO LOOK AT THE GAME FILM, WE KNOW WE PLAYED
LESS THAN OUR BEST - - - BUT WE "HUNG ON" WITH
<u>DAMNED GOOD SPIRIT</u> WHEN THE GOING WAS TOUGH. <u>JUST
THAT SAVED US</u>!

OUR PERFORMANCE WAS LACKING IN <u>BASIC EXECUTION</u>
- - - BASIC FUNDAMENTAL THINGS WE <u>CAN DO</u> AND <u>MUST
DO</u> IF WE ARE TO WIN OVER TOUGH COMPETITION
CONSISTENTLY.

WE HARP! "GIVE US A FULL 4 SECOND INTERVAL." IT
WAS MUGGY - - - IT WAS WARM - - - BUT GREATNESS
MUST COME FROM OVERCOMING "ADVERSITY." THAT IS THE
WAY IT IS! GOOD THINGS DON'T COME EASILY.

TWO FUMBLES - - - TWO TURNOVER INTERCEPTIONS
- - - AND MISSED EXECUTION MADE US <u>VERY</u> AVERAGE.
WE GAVE <u>INDIVIDUAL EFFORT</u>, BUT NOT COORDINATED AT
THE SAME TIME FOR OUR BEST EFFORT.

DON'T EVER MISUNDERSTAND, WE WON - - - WE'RE
HAPPY BUT NOT SATISFIED. NOW IS THE TIME TO PERFECT
THE DETAILS - - - BEFORE A DAY COMES WHEN EVERY
INCH AND EVERY ANGLE WILL WEIGH THE OUTCOME.

MSU - - - WILL BE HERE "ON FIRE." THEY ARE
NOTORIOUS FOR TRYING TO PUNISH PLAYERS. DEPEND ON
IT, EXPECT IT. PREPARE FOR IT. WE MUST IMPROVE
- - - LEARN - - - REFINE - - - POLISH AND PLAY
ANOTHER HARD—NOSED GAME.

THIS IS ALL THERE IS - - - ONE GAME AT A TIME.
THE GAME OF GREATEST IMPORTANCE NOW, IS MICHIGAN
STATE. NORTHWESTERN AND PURDUE ARE LONG GONE.

GET READY - - - ENJOY THE WIN, BUT WORK TO
CORRECT THE ERRORS. A SEASON IS NEVER MOTIONLESS.
YOU EITHER PROGRESS OR REGRESS. THE CHAMPION NEVER
WILTS. HE KEEPS ON KEEPING ON!

BEAT MICHIGAN STATE!!!!!!!!!

FINAL *The Phantom*

NOTRE DAME – 14   MICHIGAN STATE – 10

NOTRE DAME VS RICE
10/13/73, GAME #4

"THE PHANTOM SPEAKS"

WHAT - - - IS THERE THAT IS MORE EMPTY THAN THE
SPOKEN WORD?
* <u>PEOPLE NEVER LISTEN</u> OR <u>HEED</u>!
* <u>"NO GAME IS EASY"</u>
* <u>"EVERYONE GETS UP FOR NOTRE DAME"</u>
* <u>"A GAME IS SIXTY MINUTES"</u>
* <u>"CONDITIONING - - - LACK OF IT MAKES COWARDS
  OF US ALL"</u>
* <u>"NO GAME IS MORE IMPORTANT THAN THE ONE YOU
  ARE PLAYING!!!"</u>

DOES ANYONE EVER BECOME WISE ENOUGH TO LISTEN
WITHOUT HAVING TO BE BURNED AND TAINTED BY SCARS?

THE OFFENSE PLAYED 30 MINUTES WORTH. THEY HAD
<u>FIVE TURNOVERS</u>.

THEY DID NOT PERFORM AND RESPOND AND REACT AS A
TEAM.

DEFENSE WAS SUPER!

OFFENSE - - - WAS NOT INTENSE.

ALL THAT WE DID - - - WAS WIN. THAT IS
INFINITELY BETTER THAN PLAYING WELL AND LOSING
- - - BUT HERE IS THE <u>RUB</u>.

RICE WAS OFF - - - THEY WILL PREPARE FOR 2
WEEKS FOR NOTRE DAME. THEY HAVE OUR FILM AND OUR
TENDENCIES. WE PLAY THEM IN THEIR BACKYARD. THEY
WILL COME CLAWING AND SCRATCHING AT YOU. "THE
FASTEST GUN LIVES IN THE KNOWLEDGE THAT EVERYONE
REALLY THINKS HE'S FASTER."

THEY'LL TRY US! IF WE PLAY FOR 30 MINUTES, IF
WE THROW INTERCEPTIONS, IF WE FUMBLE, IF WE DON'T
HUSTLE ON EVERY PLAY - - - AND PLAY WITH
SPONTANEOUS ENTHUSIASM - - - WE CANNOT POSSIBLE
EXPECT TO WIN!

ONE GREAT SECRET OF GREAT TEAMS. NO ONE PRIZES
INDIVIDUAL ACHIEVEMENT OR PRAISE OVER TEAM VICTORY.
THE ONE OVERWHELMING "CONCEPT" OF "LET <u>US</u> WIN"
DOMINATES GREAT TEAMS.

THERE ARE PLAYERS ON CERTAIN PLAYS - - - THAT

DON'T CARRY THEIR LOAD. THEY DON'T <u>ADD</u> TO US —
THEY SUBTRACT. PERFORMANCE <u>IS</u> ALL THAT SHOWS.
OFFENSIVELY WE LAID <u>EGGS</u>.

   ONE SAVING FACTOR, WE DIDN'T <u>LOSE</u> THE <u>GAME</u>
- - - GOD HELP US, BEFORE IT COSTS US ONE.

   THE MICHIGAN STATE OFFENSE - - - CRIED IN UNISON
ON THEIR SIDELINE "DEFENSE, DEFENSE." THEIR DEFENSE
DID THE SAME: "OFFENSE, OFFENSE." THEY WERE OF ONE
MIND - - - DEDICATED, INTENT - - - FIRED UP. THEY
PLAYED HARD-NOSED AND HEADS UP. THEIR FIRE ALMOST
COST US A GAME. THE NOTRE DAME OFFENSE SHOULD
REALLY THANK OUR <u>DEFENSE</u>. THEY SAVED THE DAY.

   GET YOURSELF SET FOR STILL ANOTHER TASK. THE
PRICE IS STEEP, BUT THE REWARDS ARE GREAT. KEEP
<u>PROVING</u> THAT <u>YOU</u> PERSONALLY ARE WORTHY TO START
- - - TO <u>PERFORM,</u> TO BE PART OF NOTRE DAME'S
FIGHTING IRISH. GREAT ATHLETES - - - LIKE GREAT
THINGS - - - ARE MADE NOT SO MUCH FROM TALENT - -
- GUT <u>RARE</u> DESIRE - - - BURNING HEARTS!!!

   YOU CHOOSE THIS PATH - - - AND YOU'LL ONLY
TRAVEL IT ONCE. LET'S GET IT ALL RIGHT. AND - - -
              BEAT RICE!!!!!

The Phantom

FINAL
NOTRE DAME – 28   RICE – 0

NOTRE DAME VS ARMY
10/20/73, GAME #5

"THE PHANTOM SPEAKS"

ONE OF THE THRILLS OF BEATING RICE WAS THAT WE REALLY PUT TOGETHER A UNITED EFFORT. NO ONE WAS LAX OR DULL; WE CAME TO PLAY AS A TEAM AND HUSTLED! WE BEAT A GOOD TEAM UNDER TOUGH CIRCUMSTANCES FOR OUR 4TH WIN.

OUR PROBLEMS BECOME "INDIVIDUALIZED" EACH WEEK. SINCE KNOWLEDGE IS ARMOR AND FOREWARNED IS SOMETIMES FOREARMED, IT IS IMPERATIVE TO UNDERSTAND THE TOTAL SITUATION.

ARMY WILL BE IN THEIR OWN HOME FIELD, IN FRONT OF THEIR CADETS. THEY JUST CAME OFF A FRUSTRATING AND HUMILIATING DEFEAT TO PENN STATE. THIS IS EXACTLY THE POINT LAST YEAR WHERE MISSOURI LOST A 62 TO 0 GAME TO NEBRASKA — AND THEN UPSET US. INTENSITY - - - IS PERHAPS THE GREATEST SINGLE TRAIT OF A GREAT COMPETITOR. IT MATTERS NOT WHO YOU PLAY - - - YOU HAVE TO BE MENTALLY PREPARED TO SELL OUT WITH ALL THE INTENSITY WINNING DEMANDS. GIVE CREDIT - - - THAT ELEVEN ARMY MEN - - - WILL BE DOING THEIR VERY BEST AGAINST YOU IN A HIGHLY SPIRITED - - - COURAGEOUS WAY. THEY HAVE NOTHING TO LOSE.

IN MAJOR COLLEGE FOOTBALL ANY TEAM - - - ANYWHERE - - - ANYTIME CAN LICK ANYONE. WE HAVE TO ALLOW THAT THIS CAN HAPPEN IN ALL CIRCUMSTANCES AND REMEMBER THAT <u>NO GAME</u> IS MORE <u>IMPORTANT</u> THAN THE ONE WE ARE PLAYING.

DEFENSE - - - NIEHAUS IS PROBABLY LOST FOR A SEASON, BUT DEFENSE IS BUILT ON TEAM PLAY AND THOUGH WE WILL SORELY MISS HIM - - - WE MUST - - - WILL - - - CAN - - - TAKE UP THE SLACK!

OFFENSE - - - WITHOUT TURNOVERS WE COULD HAVE BEEN AWESOME VERSUS RICE OR ANYBODY. THIS IS CONCENTRATION - - - AWARENESS OF THE BALL - - - TOTAL COMMITMENT TO WHAT WE'RE DOING - - - HANG ON TO THE BALL AND EXECUTE THE PROPER WAYS TO DO THINGS. IT ENDS HERE — NO MORE TURNOVERS - - -

JUST ABSOLUTELY MAKE UP YOUR MIND IT ISN'T GOING TO
BE YOU THAT ALLOWS IT!

LASTLY - - - LET'S PLAY A SOLID GAME - - -
WHERE ALL TEAMMATES CAN ENJOY THE OPPORTUNITY TO
PLAY. LET'S GO UP TO BEAT ARMY WITH CLASS.

ANYONE CAN BREAK A SINGLE TOOTHPICK - - - HAVE
YOU EVER TRIED BREAKING 22 OF THEM TOGETHER?

THAT'S THE SECRET - - - DON'T EVER LOSE SIGHT
OF IT!

BEAT ARMY!!!

The Phantom

FINAL
NOTRE DAME – 62   ARMY – 3

NOTRE DAME VS SOUTHERN CALIFORNIA
10/27/73, GAME #6

"THE PHANTOM SPEAKS"

IN THE EARLY SEASON I STATED A TRUTH "ALL ENERGY FOLLOWS THOUGHT."

BEFORE ANYTHING EVER COMES TO A REALITY IT MUST FORM AS A THOUGHT FIRST. PRAYER WORKS THIS WAY ALSO - - - IT IS A THOUGHT - - - PROJECTED ALONG WITH WORK TOWARDS A GOAL.

I DON'T FEEL THE NEED OF GETTING AN UPSET STOMACH FOR 5 DAYS BEFORE WE PLAY SOUTHERN CAL. I SEE IT DIFFERENTLY - - - WE MUST APPROACH THE PREPARATION AND THE GAME WITH ONE UNITED THOUGHT. IF WE PUT ALL OUR MINDS INTO A SINGLE-MINDED THOUGHT - - - AND WE WORK HARD - - - AND WE PLAY WITH EMOTION - - - UNITED - - - I HOLD, WE WILL WIN!

I CHOOSE NOT TO SEE IT ANY OTHER WAY - - - BECAUSE ANY OTHER WAY IS NOT POSITIVE. POSITIVE WILL BE OUR STRENGTH. WE ARE GOING TO DO IT! START MONDAY - - - WE — ARE - - - GOING TO GO AFTER SOUTHERN CAL.

WE HAVE TO PREPARE WITH A FULL ATTENTIVE MIND. WE HAVE TO HUSTLE AND PERFORM AND EXECUTE AT OUR BEST. LET'S PROJECT THE THOUGHT OF A SOUND GAME - - - NO TURNOVERS - - - NO MISCUES OR MISSED ASSIGNMENTS, NO LET UPS EMOTIONALLY OR PHYSICALLY.

THEY CAN BE HAD - - - AND WE CAN AND WILL DO IT.

AGAINST ARMY - - - WE WORRIED THE WORRY OF ALL TEAMS. WHEN EXACTLY THE SAME NUMBER OF PLAYERS ARE PITTED AGAINST THE SAME NUMBER, WHEN THEY HAVE RELATIVE SIZE AND SPEED - - - WHEN THEY HAVE SIMILAR BACKGROUND IN TRADITION AND COACHING. WHAT IS THE DIFFERENCE? THE DIFFERENCE IS STRICTLY IN THE "DESIRE" ONE GROUP HAS OVER THE OTHER.

NOTICE I SAID "ONE GROUP," NOT ONE INDIVIDUAL.

TAKE THE GREATEST PLAYER WHO EVER PLAYED - - - ALLOW ME TO PICK ELEVEN INTERHALL PLAYERS AND ELEVEN TO ONE - - - I'LL WIN.

WHEN WE TAKE THE FIELD VERSUS SOUTHERN CAL - - -
IF WE ARE OF <u>ONE MIND</u> AND HAVE <u>ONE GOAL</u>, AND PLAY
A FULL 60 MINUTES WITH A <u>FULL NOTRE DAME HEART</u>
- - - WE HAVE GOT TO EMERGE THE VICTOR!
   SOUTHERN CAL HAS HAD ONE COMING FOR A LONG, LONG
TIME. THEY'VE OUTSIZED AND OUT-INDIVIDUALIZED MANY
- - - BUT WE WILL OUT-<u>TEAM</u> THEM. WE WILL BE THE
GIANT KILLERS - - - IF WE GO AFTER IT.
   NO GAME IS AS IMPORTANT AS THE GAME YOU ARE
PLAYING. TIME HAS COME TO QUIT THINKING ABOUT IT
- - - QUIT TALKING ABOUT IT (WORDS ARE EMPTY) AND
GO DO IT!!!!
       BEAT SOUTHERN CAL!!!!!!!!!!!!!

The Phantom

FINAL
NOTRE DAME – 23   SOUTHERN CALIFORNIA – 14

NOTRE DAME VS NAVY
11/3/73, GAME #7

"THE PHANTOM SPEAKS"

"GIVE A BEGGAR A HORSE AND HE'LL RIDE IT TO DEATH." YOU CANNOT SAVOR THE 6TH WIN - - - IT IS OVER. (UNLIKE THE BEGGAR - - - WE MUST KNOW THIS AND START ANEW WITH #7.) NO ONE EVER WON A GAME BECAUSE THEY WERE SUPPOSED TO WIN IT.

THE S.C. WIN WAS ABSOLUTELY GREAT! IT IS THE EVIDENCE AND TESTIMONY THAT STANDS ALWAYS; "EMOTION" - - - WHEN UNITED - - - WHEN PREPARED, IS DIFFICULT TO DENY!!

THE DEFENSE WAS REALLY TOGETHER! OFFENSE KEPT THE BALL 40 MINUTES - - - KEPT THE DRIVES GOING - - - - ATE UP THE CLOCK - - - AND PUT POINTS ON THE BOARD. WE DID WHAT WE HAD TO DO TO WIN. WE BEAT A GREAT TEAM OF INDIVIDUALS WITH GREAT "TEAMWORK", UNIFIED AND SOLID.

WHERE DO WE GO FROM HERE? WHAT IS NORMAL? THE BIG LETDOWN!? HERE IS FAULTY REASONING. "WE BEAT SOUTHERN CAL - - - THEREFORE - - - ETC." TO HELL WITH THEREFORE - - - WE PLAY NAVY. WE'VE JUST INCITED THEM. WE JUST FIXED THEIR RESOLVE AND MAPPED THEIR PLAN. THEY WILL SHOOT FOR US - - - AS WE DID OUR BIG BIG OPPONENT. NOW - - - WE ARE THE BIG OPPONENT.

NAVY PRESENTS SEVERAL PROBLEMS. THEIR OFFENSIVE TEAM IS VERY EXPLOSIVE. THEY ARE BIGGER OR AS BIG AS SOUTHERN CAL. THEY PLAY SPIRITED FOOTBALL, ARE SUPER-CONDITIONED AND NEVER QUIT - - - THEY, TOO, ARE FULL OF "UNIFIED PRIDE." YOU KNOW THE "IRONY"? IN THE HANDS OF AN OPPONENT, UNIFIED PRIDE IS DANGEROUS! WE KNOW - - - WE'VE JUST EXPERIENCED IT! WHAT WAS ONCE OUR ADVANTAGE VERSUS S.C. NOW BECOMES OUR OPPONENTS' WEAPON. THEY WILL BE INSPIRED AGAINST US.

THOUGH WE WON THE BATTLE OF USC - - - THE WAR IS STILL ON - - - AND WE HAVE REMAINING BATTLES TO WIN. ONE GAME IS NOT A SEASON, ONLY ONE BATTLE.

NAVY'S DEFENSE WILL CLAW AND SWARM. THIS IS

THEIR STRENGTH! NAVY'S TAILBACK IS DANGEROUS.
THEY'LL FIELD AN ALL-SENIOR TEAM WHICH SCORED 21
POINTS VERSUS THE IRISH A YEAR AGO.
WE KNOW WHERE WE ARE - - - AND WHERE WE WANT TO
GO. WE ALSO KNOW WHAT WE MUST DO TO WIN!
    #1. PLAY THIS & REMEMBER "NO GAME IS MORE
IMPORTANT THAN NAVY"
    #2. TO BEAT SOUTHERN CAL AND BE UPSET BECAUSE OF
THINKING BACK AND NOT PREPARING FOR THE NEW
OPPONENT - - - IS <u>COMMONPLACE</u>, WE MUST BE UNCOMMON.
    #3. NOTHING HAPPENS BY ITSELF - - - PEOPLE MAKE
THINGS HAPPEN - - - AGAIN - - - UNITED - - - IN
TUNE - - - PREPARE - - - EXECUTE - - - AND MAKE IT
HAPPEN.
               BEAT NAVY!!!!

The Phantom

FINAL
NOTRE DAME – 44   NAVY – 7

NOTRE DAME VS PITTSBURGH
11/10/73, GAME #8

"THE PHANTOM SPEAKS"

GET READY - - - GET SET! PITTSBURGH IS WAITING. WE WILL WALK INTO A REAL HORNETS' NEST!!!

MAKE NO MISTAKE: PITTSBURGH IS BIG - - - THEY ARE PHYSICAL - - - THEY ARE VASTLY IMPROVED. THEY HAVE A COACH WHO HAS BROUGHT IN 82 FRESHMAN. THEY HAVE DEPTH! THEY HAVE OPENLY SAID THEY WILL KNOCK US OFF FROM THE UNDEFEATED LIST.

THEY HAVE SAID THAT CLEMENTS IS NOT THE EQUAL OF DANIELS. PENICK IS NOT THE EQUAL OF DORSETT. I PROMISE - - - IT WILL BE A DOG FIGHT. WE WILL HAVE TO BE AT OUR BEST.

PITT. FEELS VENGEANCE TOWARD ANY OF OUR PENNSYLVANIA PLAYERS, ESPECIALLY OUR QB. IT WILL BE HOSTILE AND TOUGH ON ARTIFICIAL TURF IN THEIR STADIUM.

THERE IS ONE THING THEY OVERLOOKED. SURE - - - THERE WAS AN EMOTIONAL LETDOWN FOR NAVY - - - (BUT THAT'S HISTORY - - - WE'RE OVER THAT!) SURE - - - THEY ARE IMPROVED (BUT THEY ARE STILL INDIVIDUALS). THEY DON'T REALIZE THE STRENGTH OF CHARACTER - - - THE TEAM BOND - - - THE "ONENESS" OF THE IRISH.

THEY REPRESENT ONE BIG STUMBLING BLOCK IN OUR PATH.

WE MUST PLAY "UP." WE MUST BE SHARP - - - EXECUTE - - - NO ERRORS - - - NO BREAKDOWNS OR TURNOVERS.

WE MUST REALLY GO AFTER PITT. IF WE ARE TO WIN IT. 7 NAVY FUMBLES IF REPEATED WILL LOSE US THE PITT GAME. WE MUST - - - RE-DO- - - RE-KINDLE - - - AND REALLY GET TUNED IN TO ONE GOAL - - - ONE DRIVE - - - ONE RESULT - - - BEAT PITT!!!

THE PITT COACH HAS BALLYHOOED THIS GAME. HE WANTS A REPUTATION - - - AT OUR EXPENSE. WE ARE TO BE THE SACRIFICIAL GOAT ON THEIR HOME ALTAR.

FIRE UP - - - TAKE STOCK OF THE SITUATION AND REMIND THEM THEY'RE NOT PLAYING "KIDS" - - -

THEY'RE PLAYING NOTRE DAME. LET US TATTOO THEM WITH
THAT THOUGHT TO LIVE WITH.
BEAT PITT!!!!!

The Phantom

FINAL
NOTRE DAME – 31   PITTSBURGH – 10

NOTRE DAME VS AIR FORCE
11/22/73, GAME #9

"THE PHANTOM SPEAKS"

PITTSBURGH REPRESENTED #8 IN OUR LIST OF GOALS
TOWARDS A NATIONAL CHAMPIONSHIP. IT IS A FACT —
THERE ARE NO EASY OPPONENTS! WHEN THEY PLAY US
- - - THEY ARE PSYCHED — PREPARED — READY. TO PLAY
WELL AGAINST US INSURES STARDOM - - - "BACK OF THE
WEEK," "LINEMAN OR LINEBACKER" ON AP OR UP
LISTINGS. UNLIKE OTHER ROADS TRAVELED, OUR PATH
DOES NOT SMOOTH OUT, IT WILL GET A LITTLE ROUGHER.

WE ARE FACING AIR FORCE. AIR FORCE, WHEN THEY
WERE "UP" AND "RIGHT," PLAYED PENN STATE OFF THEIR
FEET AND LED THEM NEARLY FOR A HALF THEY LOST 19
TO 10 BY A LONG PASS.

LET'S TAKE STOCK - - - THEY HAVE NOTHING BUT US
THAT CAN SALVAGE THEIR SEASON - - - BUT NOTRE DAME
APPEARS AT HOME IN 1973 FOR THE LAST TIME. OUR
SENIORS - - - WILL PLAY THEIR LAST HOME GAME ON
NOTRE DAME TURF - - - EVER.

EINSTEIN ONCE HYPOTHESIZED "TIME DOES NOT MOVE,
BUT MEN MOVE THRU TIME!"

A MORE DOWN-TO-EARTH THEORY: "LIFE IS LIKE
TOOTHPASTE, WHEN YOU SQUEEZE IT OUT OF THE TUBE,
THERE IS NO STUFFING IT BACK IN!"

AND STILL ANOTHER BEER COMMERCIAL SINGS OUT,
"GET ALL THE GUSTO YOU CAN BECAUSE, WE ONLY GO
AROUND ONCE!"

THERE IS A GRAIN OF TRUTH IN ALL OF THIS. WE
HAVE AN OPPORTUNITY TO BE PART OF SOMETHING VERY
SPECIAL. WHAT WE ARE SHOOTING FOR FOLLOWS ONE ALL
OF HIS LIFE. WE WANT TO BE THE ULTIMATE - - - THE
CHAMPIONS.

CONSIDER THE STRUGGLE MADE TO ARRIVE AT AN
ELEVEN ROUND WORLD CHAMPIONSHIP FIGHT - - -
CONSIDER HAVING WON 8 ROUNDS - - - CONSIDER GETTING
CARELESS - - - OR OVERCONFIDENT — OR TIRED — OR
BORED — JUST BEFORE THE 9TH, 10TH AND 11TH ROUNDS.

THE CHAMPION - - - THE TRUE ONE, HAS ALREADY
MENTALLY ACKNOWLEDGED THAT EVERYONE TIRES - - -

GETS OVERCONFIDENT - - - IS BORED, BUT THAT HIS OPPORTUNITY IS RIGHT NOW AND THAT HE ABSOLUTELY WON'T AND CAN'T TRAVEL THIS ROAD AGAIN. HE TELLS HIMSELF - - - "NO WAY BABY - - - AM I GOING TO SHORT-CHANGE MYSELF BY NOT BEING READY!"

AND THERE IT IS - - - LET'S BE READY - - - LET'S LET OUR LAST TIME "SENIORS" CLOSE OUT NOTRE DAME HOME GAMES WITH A RESOUNDING VICTORY — LET'S BEAT AIR FORCE IN OUR 9TH ROUND. AND ONE LAST THING; CHAMPIONS ARE <u>NOT BORN</u> OR <u>MADE</u>, THEY MAKE THEMSELVES!!! GOOD LUCK.

BEAT AIR FORCE!!!!

The Phantom

FINAL
NOTRE DAME – 48   AIR FORCE – 15

NOTRE DAME VS MIAMI (FLA)
12/1/1973, GAME #10

"THE PHANTOM SPEAKS"

MANY TIMES WE HAVE KNOCKED AT THE PERFECT 10 &
0 SEASON. IN TEN YEARS IT HAS EVADED US. WEATHER
FACTORS - - - INJURIES TOWARDS A SEASON'S END
- - - MORALE - - - TIRED OR EMOTIONALLY DRAINED
- - - WHATEVER PAST REASONS MAY HAVE BEEN, IT HAS
NOT BEEN DONE.

I BELIEVE WE CAN DO IT! WE ARE PHYSICALLY PRETTY
GOOD. WE WILL OVERCOME THE WEATHER FACTOR. MORALE
AND SPIRIT OF THE 1973 BALL CLUB HAS BEEN
SPECTACULAR. I'VE NOT SEEN MANY TEAMS LESS SELFISH.

MIAMI IS A VERY <u>FORMIDABLE</u> OPPONENT. THEY ARE
VERY BIG AND VERY QUICK. THEY HAVE PLAYED THE CLASS
TEAMS IN THE COUNTRY AND DONE IT WELL. DEFENSE IS
THEIR 1ST STRENGTH. THEY FEEL THEY CAN DEFINITELY
SHUT OFF OUR RUN GAME. THEIR SCOUT SAID SO OVER
PUBLIC MEDIA!

OFFENSIVELY THEY STATE PITT AND SOUTHERN CAL RAN
ON US, AS WELL AS PASSED ON OUR SECONDARY.

THIS WILL BE A TOUGH AND SEVERE TEST. WE MUST
PLAY ERROR FREE. NO TURNOVERS, GOOD KICKING GAME,
TOUGH SWARMING DEFENSE - - - AND SUSTAINED
OFFENSIVE DRIVES WITH MAXIMUM EFFORT. NONE OF THIS
IS NEW - - - BUT THAT IS HOW WE GOT TO 9 & 0. WE
MUST REPEAT IT! MIAMI IS PROBABLY THE 2ND BEST TEAM
ON OUR SCHEDULE.

GET READY FOR A HARD KNOCKING CONTEST AND SUCK
UP YOUR BELLIES FOR A "DOG FIGHT."

ONE THING TO REMEMBER - - - WE ARE A DAMNED
GOOD TEAM, WELL DISCIPLINED AND PHYSICALLY CAPABLE
WITH HIGH MORALE. WE ARE NOTRE DAME, NOT AS
INDIVIDUALS, BUT AS A "TEAM" - - - "ONE." MIAMI
CANNOT "OUT-WANT US" - - - "OUT-HIT US" - - -
"OUT-FIGHT US" IF WE REFUSE TO LET IT HAPPEN.

LET'S GO NOTRE DAME - - - WITH ONLY ONE THOUGHT
PERVADING.

WE WANT IT AND MEAN TO GET IT! LET'S GO DOWN
AND <u>BEAT MIAMI</u>!!!!!!!

The Phantom

FINAL
NOTRE DAME – 44   MIAMI (FLA) – 0

1974

NOTRE DAME VS GEORGIA TECH
9/9/74, GAME #1

"THE PHANTOM SPEAKS"

THERE ARE TIMES WHEN MERE WORDS SMACK OF "CORNY SOUNDS." THINGS ARE "CORNY" BECAUSE THEY ARE <u>OLD</u>. IF THEY ARE OLD - - - THERE MUST BE A KERNEL OF TRUTH IN THEM TO HAVE BEEN AROUND SO LONG.

ONE WORD THAT FITS THE BILL IS <u>TRADITION</u>. TO LESS KNOWLEDGEABLE PEOPLE OR TOO YOUNG OR SOPHISTICATED PEOPLE, <u>TRADITION</u> IS AN INTANGIBLE PHRASE.

TO NOTRE DAME'S FOOTBALL TEAM, THE WORD SUMMARIZES ALL THAT WE HOLD DEAR. IT MEANS NO MEMBER OF THE TEAM IS GREATER THAN THE TEAM. IT MEANS THAT MEN WITH COMMON GOALS, ALL AIMED AT ONE OBJECTIVE, WILL RARELY BOW TO DEFEAT.

TRADITION MEANS - - - WE WILL FIELD A TEAM OF SELFLESS PEOPLE WHO BY DOING SO BECOME BIGGER AS INDIVIDUALS. IT MEANS SUPERBLY CONDITIONED, WELL-PREPARED, AND MENTALLY TOUGH NOTRE DAME TEAMS <u>TRADITIONALLY</u> - - -

1. NEVER GET INTIMIDATED!
2. NEVER GET OUT-HUSTLED OR OUT-FOUGHT.
3. ALWAYS COMMAND THE RESPECT OF THE OPPONENT BECAUSE THEY REPRESENT THE - - - CLASS OF COLLEGE FOOTBALL.

OTHERS HAVE PAID THEIR DUES TO LEAVE YOU THIS TRADITION. 1973 AND ALL THE SEASONS BEFORE ARE OVER. ONLY 1974 COUNTS RIGHT NOW - - - ONE GAME AT A TIME.

TO THE 1974 "FIGHTING IRISH" THE CLOAK OF GLORIOUS TRADITION IS AWARDED TO YOU — WEARING IT IS NOT EASY, BUT THEN ALL THINGS HIGHLY PRIZED - - - NEVER COME EASY.

GA. TECH - - - IN THE SOUTH, IN THE HEAT - - - THE NIGHT - - - THE HOSTILE CROWD, CAN MAKE EACH MAN FEEL ALONE. OUR OPEN SECRET HAS ALWAYS BEEN - - - "WE'RE NEVER ALONE." WE'RE A TEAM — BONDED TOGETHER AND UNIFIED. OUR STRENGTH STEMS FROM UNITY. AS A TEAM - - - WE WILL OVERCOME THE

OBSTACLES . . . STRENGTH STEMS FROM UNITY. AS A
TEAM - - - WE WILL OVERCOME THE OBSTACLES . . .
   NATIONAL T.V. & GA. TECH ARE EARLY AND STRONG
TESTS - - - NOT IMPOSSIBLE ONES!!!
   LET'S GET OUR FIRST WIN <u>TOGETHER</u>!! GOOD LUCK &
GO IRISH!!! MEN OF NOTRE DAME!!!

The Phantom

FINAL
NOTRE DAME – 31   GEORGIA TECH – 7

NOTRE DAME VS NORTHWESTERN
9/21/74, GAME #2

"THE PHANTOM SPEAKS"

WHEN THE "FIGHTING IRISH" ASSEMBLED FOR THEIR LAST REMINDERS, AGAINST GEORGIA TECH; WHEN THEY KNEELED EN MASSE, REACHING OUT TO TOUCH SOMEONE ELSE ON "OUR TEAM,"' THE UNITY OF TEAM INTENTION AND DEDICATION TOLD ME WE WOULD NOT BE BEATEN EASILY!

HAVING PREPARED PHYSICALLY, MENTALLY, AND EMOTIONALLY, ONLY THE EXECUTION AND EFFORT REMAINED TO BRING US OUR FIRST 1974 SEASON VICTORY.

EVERYONE WE PLAY WILL RISE UP TO THEIR HIGHEST POINT FOR US. THIS IS A TOUGH REALITY THAT IS REALLY A HIGH FORM OF COMPLIMENT.

IT WOULD BE SHAKY IF WE WERE NOT AWARE OF IT . . . BUT WE ARE . . . AND THIS KNOWLEDGE FOREARMS US NOT TO RELAX AND NEVER TO UNDERESTIMATE THE OPPONENT.

THE FIRST WIN WAS A TRIBUTE TO THE OFFENSIVE AND DEFENSIVE PREP TEAMS. IT WAS THE BIG "D" COMING OF AGE ON A GOAL-LINE STAND. IT WAS AN OFFENSE THAT PLAYED TO OVERCOME OBSTACLES . . . FOR A FULL AND COMPLETE 60 MINUTES. WITHIN THE GREAT TEAM VICTORY WERE MAGNIFICENT INDIVIDUAL PLAYS THAT SPURRED AND IGNITED THE ENTIRE TEAM. THIS IS THE THRILL IN FOOTBALL . . . TO OVERCOME ALL THAT OPPOSES WITH THE TENACITY OF EFFORT AND THE COOPERATION OF MANY MINDS AND HEARTS "TUNED IN" TO A FINAL GOAL.

WE HAVE TWO RATHER WORN SAYINGS AT NOTRE DAME. (1) THAT "WE" HAVE NO BREAKING POINT! (BEHIND BY 30 OR AHEAD BY 30 - - - WE'RE COMING AFTER YOU WITH THE SAME DEGREE OF INTENSITY BECAUSE A TEAM THAT WON'T LET ITSELF BE BEATEN, CANNOT BE BEATEN!) (2) NO GAME IS AS IMPORTANT AS THE ONE YOU ARE PLAYING! (WHAT WENT BEFORE - - - OTHER GAMES, AND OTHER TIMES, WON'T HELP NOW! A LONG LOOK DOWN THE ROAD AT AN ARCH-RIVAL - - - WILL NOT HELP ON THE PARTICULAR DAY OF A CONTEST WITH A DIFFERENT OPPONENT. THE GAME WE ARE MOST INVOLVED WITH - - -

THE MOST IMPORTANT CONTEST IN THE WORLD TO ALL OF US HERE AND NOW - - - IS THE ONE WE ARE GOING TO PLAY. IN THIS CASE NORTHWESTERN'S WILDCATS.)

EACH MAN LEARNS TO BELIEVE IN HIMSELF AND THE THINGS HE BELONGS TO. WE ALL BELONG TO THIS 1974 NOTRE DAME TEAM. WE MUST THEREFORE BELIEVE THAT OUR SMALL PARTS MAY BECOME BIG PARTS IN THE OVERALL SUCCESS. WE CANNOT WAVER OR WEAKEN, ONLY PREPARE.

SOMEONE ONCE SAID THAT "SUCCESS IS WHEN PREPARATION MEETS OPPORTUNITY. MANY PEOPLE NEVER FIND IT BECAUSE IT IS HIDDEN UNDER HARD WORK." IF THE GOOD THINGS AND MOMENTS OF LIFE COME WITH WORK, LET US WORK WITH JOY! NOTHING IS SADDER THAN "IT MIGHT HAVE BEEN." FEW THINGS ARE MORE GRAND THAN "WE DID IT." LET'S DO IT TO NORTHWESTERN!!

BEAT THE WILDCATS!!!!

The Phantom

FINAL
NOTRE DAME – 49   NORTHWESTERN – 3

NOTRE DAME VS PURDUE
9/27/74, GAME #3

"THE PHANTOM SPEAKS"

HUNGER, NOT PHYSICAL HUNGER FOR FOOD, BUT TO
ACHIEVE AND SUCCEED - - - MARKS ALL GREAT EFFORT.
IN THE FIRST HALF OF THE NORTHWESTERN GAME - - -
WE PLAYED WITH ONLY THE MOTIONS - - - NOT THE
EMOTIONS. WE DIDN'T BLOCK WITH INTENSITY OR SUSTAIN
OR GRIP THE BALL. A BETTER TEAM THAN NORTHWESTERN
COULD HAVE CAPITALIZED ON OUR "DOWN" PLAY. WE WERE
LUCKY!

WE PLAY PURDUE AT HOME THIS WEEK. PURDUE WITH A
LOSS TO WISCONSIN AND A TIE WITH MIAMI OF OHIO
- - - ENTERS THE ARENA WITH LITTLE TO LOSE AND ALL
TO GAIN. WE FACE THEIR UNDERDOG ROLE - - - THEIR
REPUTATION AS SPOILERS, THEIR WAY TO MAKE AMENDS.
WE CANNOT ALLOW TURNOVERS. THEY ARE DEATH TO A
VICTORY.

WHEN I THINK OF VICTORY AND WINNING - - - AND I
HAVE KNOWN THE OPPOSITE END OF THIS - - -; I LIKE
WINNING BETTER.

AS SOPHIE TUCKER ONCE REMARKED, "I'VE BEEN RICH
AND I'VE BEEN POOR; RICH IS BETTER!" AND SO WITH
WINNING. TO WIN AND STILL RECALL THE BITTER TOTAL
LOSS OF A LOSING EFFORT - - - MAYBE THE FACTOR
THAT CAUSES EMOTIONAL HUNGER, BUT MEMORY WILL
SUFFICE! WE ARE A TEAM - - - WE MUST PERFORM AS
ONE. EACH MAN MUST SURELY DO HIS PART AND DO IT
WITH HIS BEST EFFORT.

FOOTBALL IS A GREAT GAME, BECAUSE NO ONE AND
ESPECIALLY NO TEAM CAN BE TAKEN FOR GRANTED.

IF A TEAM WERE SUPPOSED TO WIN OR SUPPOSED TO
LOSE — WHY DO WE BOTHER TO PLAY? THE ELEMENTS ARE
THE SAME; GREAT CHALLENGE, GREAT COMPETITION, GREAT
PREPARATION - - - AND GREAT FINAL EXECUTION - - -
DONE WITH A HUNGER TO WIN. NO MATTER WHAT - - -
THIS NEVER CHANGES! PURDUE HAS SIZE - - - SPEED
- - - SKILLS - - - AND A GRAND INTENT TO WIN OVER
NOTRE DAME. IF IT HAPPENS EASILY OR FREQUENTLY

- - - NOTRE DAME WILL LOSE THE PINNACLE OF RESPECT
SHE HAS EARNED FROM "NOT BEING EASY."
   SO VERY FEW EVER HAVE THE CHANCE TO BE A PART
OF NOTRE DAME'S FOOTBALL HISTORY. EACH OF YOU HAS
THAT OPPORTUNITY. HOW DO YOU WANT YOUR HISTORY HERE
TO READ - - - LET IT BE SAID OF YOU - - - "THEY
PLAYED LIKE A NOTRE DAME TEAM!"
                    BEAT PURDUE!!!

The Phantom

FINAL
NOTRE DAME – 20   PURDUE – 31

NOTRE DAME VS MICHIGAN STATE
10/5/74, GAME #4

"THE PHANTOM SPEAKS"

WE WIN TOGETHER AND WE LOSE TOGETHER! THERE IS
NO POINT TO PLACE BLAME BECAUSE IT POINTS AT ALL
OF US: COACHES, OFFENSE AND DEFENSE! IT STARTS WITH
LETTING YOU LOAF THROUGH CALS OR EASING UP - - -
OR LAGGING OUT, BECAUSE OF A TINY INJURY. WE AS
COACHES LET YOU AND WE'RE WRONG. IT POINTS AT
PLAYER MENTAL ATTITUDE WHEN COACHES HAVE TO YELL TO
GET EFFORT IN PRACTICE. YOU CANNOT MANUFACTURE
ENTHUSIASM; IT IS NATURAL. WE BLEW ASSIGNMENTS
- - - AND ONE MISS SETS OFF CHAINS OF EVENTS
CAUSING PENALTIES, INTERCEPTIONS, OR TURNOVERS.
AGAIN - - - WE WON STATISTICALLY, THAT'S WHY
STATISTICS ARE FOR THE LOSING SIDE.

I HATE LOSING; ALL GREAT COMPETITORS DO! LOSING
IN ITSELF IS TOUGH ENOUGH - - - BUT TO CONTRIBUTE
TO IT BY NOT BEING TENACIOUS OR "WITH IT" HURTS
GREATLY. WE ARE BETTER THAN WE PLAYED!

DID YOU RECOGNIZE THE "HUNGER" OF PURDUE? HUNGER
IS NEVER PRESENT WHERE SELF-SATISFIED, OR PROUD, OR
SURE IS PRESENT. I JUST DESCRIBED US A WEEK AGO
. . .

IT REALLY HURTS! WHAT GAME COULD BE MORE
IMPORTANT THAN THE ONE WE WERE PLAYING?

ONE BIG POINT. IT IS A STUPID MAN OR TEAM THAT
DOES NOT LEARN FROM MISTAKES. HISTORY TELLS US YOU
ARE DOOMED TO REPEAT FORGOTTEN MISTAKES.

GRASP THIS IF YOU CAN! SURE YOU WERE 1973
NATIONAL CHAMPS. SURE, EVERYONE GOT HIGHER THAN
KITES FOR YOU, AND SURE, IT IS A FEATHER TO KNOCK
OFF NOTRE DAME. NOW YOU'VE BEEN KNOCKED OFF AND
THERE ARE ONLY TWO WAYS TO GO - - - (1) MORE OF
THE SAME (2) NONE OF THE SAME.

WE NOW FACE MICHIGAN STATE - - - UP THERE. THEY
ARE COMING OFF A LOSS. THEY HAVEN'T HAD N.D.'S
SUCCESS IN THE PAST. OUR SCOUTS SAY THEY ARE BIGGER
— TOUGHER, AND A MUCH MORE AGGRESSIVE TEAM WITH
GREATER SPEED AND SKILLS THAN PURDUE.

LET ME FOREWARN YOU. YOU WILL NEVER WITNESS A
MORE FANATICAL - - - CRAZED - - - WILD-ANTICS
- - - SOUPED-UP - - - JUICED-UP - - - TEAM THIS
SEASON THAN MSU. THERE. THEY WILL PILE YOU, MAYBE
CHEAP-SHOT YOU; HIT LATE, YELL OR CURSE AT YOU.

THEIR WHOLE IDEA IS TO OVERWHELM YOU WITH THEIR
FEROCITY. THEY'LL TRY TO INTIMIDATE YOU - - - TO
MAKE YOU BACK OFF. MOST TIMES AND WITH MOST PEOPLE
—IT WORKS. THEIR WEAKNESS IS THAT ALL THAT JAZZY
STUFF WINDS DOWN IF YOU'LL GO AFTER THEM AS THE
AGGRESSOR.

WHEN A PLAYER GETS OVERWHELMED OR WHEN HE FEELS
ALONE - - - HE BECOMES RUTTED IN MEDIOCRITY AND
PERFORMS TIMIDLY.

WE WILL HAVE TO BE MORE "TOGETHER," MORE A TRUE
TEAM OF MEN READY FOR INVADING THAT ARENA THAN WE
HAVE IN OUR 1ST THREE GAMES. NOT ONE THING WILL BE
IN OUR FAVOR. NO ONE WILL BE ON OUR SIDE. WE MUST
UNDERSTAND - - - AND DEPEND UPON ABSOLUTE AND TOTAL
UNITY. ONE GROUP OF MEN INTENSELY "TUNED IN" TO ONE
IDEA, "TO GET THE JOB DONE." GET READY FOR A TOUGH
- - - REALLY HARD HITTING AFFAIR. DON'T GET READY
THURSDAY, FRIDAY OR THE 2ND HALF OF THE GAME. THAT
WON'T BE ENOUGH. START FROM SCRATCH - - - MONDAY
AND BUILD — IT IN YOUR MIND THAT WE WON'T BE
BEATEN OR INTIMIDATED OR OUT HIT OR OUT HUSTLED.

LET'S DEPEND ON OURSELVES FIRST, BY PREPARING
WELL. WHAT WE ARE MADE OF SHOWS NOT WHEN ALL GOES
WELL (THAT'S EASY) - - - BUT WHEN THINGS GET
REALLY TOUGH. IT IS A GREAT CHALLENGE TO BOUNCE
BACK WITH "HUNGER" TO WIN.

BEAT MSU!!!!!!!!

The Phantom

FINAL
NOTRE DAME – 19   MICHIGAN STATE – 14

"THE PHANTOM SPEAKS"

IT WAS NOT A MASTERPIECE WITH CRISPLY EXECUTED
PLAYS OF PERFECTION. IT WAS MORE LIKE A SLIP HERE
AND THERE — BUT IT WAS A BEAUTIFUL TEAM VICTORY IN
THE SENSE THAT WE WERE ALL OF ONE MIND. WE WANTED
TO PLAY AND TO WIN, AND WE DID!

YOU OVERCAME THE POOR OFFICIATING, THE BAD MARKS
OF THE BALL, THE PENALTIES. OUR DEFENSE SWARMED AND
RECOVERED TWO FUMBLES TO SET UP TWO SCORES. THE
OFFENSE ATE UP TIME AND PUT POINTS ON THE BOARD
WHEN WE HAD TO. THE GREATEST SATISFACTION WAS THAT
THERE WAS NO TOTAL BREAKDOWN - - - NO TOTAL LACK
OF EFFORT. SURE - - - GUYS HAD GOOD PLAYS AND BAD
PLAYS, BUT OVERALL WE WERE TRYING LIKE HELL AGAINST
A TOUGH OPPONENT, UNDER TOUGH CIRCUMSTANCES. YOU
ARE TO BE CONGRATULATED!

WORDS ARE JUST SOUNDS IF WE REALLY DON'T LISTEN
AND RECALL - - - EMPTY WORDS - - - IF WE CHOOSE TO
IGNORE, BUT TRUTH IF WE LOOK AT THIS PHRASE IN THE
EYE. "NO WIN COMES EASILY, NOTHING WORTHWHILE
WITHOUT A STRONG AND DEDICATED SACRIFICE." FOR
SHEER EFFORT - - - WAYNE BULLOCK WAS <u>SUPER</u>. ON
DEFENSE MAHALIC AND COLLINS WERE <u>STALWARTS</u>.

LET US NEVER <u>FORGET</u> THE JOY OF WINNING AND WHAT
IT TAKES. LET US NEVER TAKE IT FOR GRANTED AGAIN.

RICE: THEY TIED LSU. THEY WERE OFF LAST WEEK,
THEY ARE A GIMMICK TEAM. THE LAST TASTE IN THE
MOUTH OF OUR HOME FANS WAS OUR HOME OPENER AGAINST
PURDUE. LET'S MAKE A DISPLAY OF THE "REAL IRISH."
LET'S GO AFTER THIS GAME TO SHOW WHAT WE CAN
REALLY GET DONE. TO QUOTE ARA - - - "WINNING ISN'T
EVERYTHING, BUT LOSING IS NOTHING - - - ZERO - - -
ZIP."

WHEN RICE STEPS ON OUR FIELD - - - LET NOTRE
DAME PLAY LIKE "NOTRE DAME." I SAW THE DIFFERENCE
IN THE MSU LOCKER ROOM. WE WERE INTENT, AGAIN
HUNGRY, CONCERNED, DEDICATED AND ENTHUSIASTIC ONE.
<u>NEVER</u> LET IT BE DIFFERENT BECAUSE THAT IS THE EDGE

THE TRUE CHAMPION HOLDS!!! EVERY N.D. COACH AND
EVERY PLAYER LEFT MSU WITH GREAT SATISFACTION - - -
NOW LET US LEAVE OUR LOCKER ROOM THAT WAY
FOREVER!!!

        BEAT RICE!!!!!!!!!!

The Phantom

FINAL
NOTRE DAME – 10   RICE – 3

NOTRE DAME VS ARMY
10/19/74, GAME #6

"THE PHANTOM SPEAKS"

SOMETIMES IT BECOMES VERY EASY TO OVERLOOK THE OBVIOUS! GAMES b INT FOR THIS SEASON. THE SECOND HALF OF THE SEASON LOOMS AS TOUGHER THAN THE FIRST. WE MUST IMPROVE AND PUT TOGETHER A REAL SURGE OF BASIC FOOTBALL IF WE ARE TO COME ON STRONG. WE HAVE NOT YET EXPLODED, NOT YET JELLED - - - NOT YET PUT IT ALL TOGETHER. TEAMS CAN GO A WHOLE SEASON WITHOUT THIS "JELLING." THAT PART OF THE PICTURE IS <u>MENTAL</u>.

MENTALLY - - - YOU MUST BE TUNED IN TO WHAT WE DO, WHEN WE DO IT, AND HOW WE WANT IT DONE. THIS IS THE ROAD TO STEADY <u>IMPROVEMENT</u>.

<u>ARMY</u> - - - THIS WEEK. THEY - - - LIKE EVERY OPPONENT WILL BE INCITED AT THEIR UNDERDOG ROLE. YOU - - - NOTRE DAME ARE EXPECTED TO <u>WIN</u>. THAT EXPECTATION DRAINS YOU OF EVER ACHIEVING SATISFACTION IF AND WHEN WE DO WIN WITH ALL OF THAT. A LESSER SATISFACTION IS BETTER - - - FAR BETTER THAN ANY KIND OF LOSS. LET'S GET BETTER - - - AND BEAT ARMY SOUNDLY, BECAUSE THEY WILL CLAW AT US IF GIVEN A CHANCE!
BEAT ARMY!!!!!!!!!

The Phantom

FINAL
NOTRE DAME – 48   ARMY – 0

NOTRE DAME VS MIAMI (FLA)
10/26/74, GAME #7

"THE PHANTOM SPEAKS"

"HOW SWEET IT IS!" NOT SO MUCH WINNING OR THE
SCORE - - - BUT THE OVERWHELMING ENTHUSIASM, THE
THRILL OF UNIFIED EFFORT, THE "PERFORMANCE WITH A
FULL HEART." IF YOU ARE PART OF THE 1974 TEAM AND
STAFF, YOU JUST WITNESSED EXHIBIT A IN PROVING THAT
"DYNAMIC ENTHUSIASM LEADS TO PHYSICAL PERFORMANCE."
YOU JUST EXPERIENCED THE SATISFACTION OF
ACHIEVEMENT AS A RESULT OF COORDINATED TEAM EFFORT.

NO OTHER FACET OF LIFE HOLDS THIS RARE
EXPERIENCE MORE PROFOUNDLY THAN COLLEGE FOOTBALL.
IT IS A PLEASURE TO RUN AND BLOCK AND TACKLE! IT
IS FUN TO SCORE AND DEFEND IN THE SUN, MUD OR
RAIN. IT IS WITHOUT A DOUBT A UNIQUE EXPERIENCE IN
TODAY'S CULTURE, TO GET INVOLVED WITH TOTAL EMOTION
AND DEDICATION.

T.V. - - - RADIO - - - PAPERS - - - THEATRES
- - - ALL CURRENTLY IDOLIZE AND MAGNIFY THE "MR.
COOL" — "THE HUSTLER WHO DID IT WITH TRICKS" - - -
"THE SMART EASY WAY." THIS IS THE POPULAR NORM THAT
THE MASS OF PEOPLE TRY TO EMULATE. HOW SAD BECAUSE
"COOL" IS <u>MEDIOCRE</u> AND "ON FIRE" IS GREATNESS!
FOOTBALL - - - DEMANDS THAT THERE IS NO EASY WAY
- - - NO WAY TO BE COOL OR ALOOF WHEN YOU'VE BEEN
KNOCKED ON YOUR DUFF. THERE IS A RAW, NAKED, HONEST
BEAUTY IN ACHIEVING PHYSICAL PERFORMANCE; THERE IS
A THRILL IN AN "ON FIRE" TEAM PLAY, THAT CANNOT BE
MATCHED BY ANY OTHER HARMONY. LET'S NEVER FORGET
THE LESSON AND WHAT MUST GO INTO IT.

ONE YEAR AGO WE SOUNDLY THRASHED A TEAM NOT
READY TO PLAY US. WE HAD MOMENTUM AND THEY DID
NOT. WE CLOSED THEIR SEASON WITH A PUNISHING 44 TO
0 LOSS. THEY REMEMBER IT WELL. IT HAS BEEN THEIR
1974 CHANT AND LOCKER ROOM SLOGAN. "REMEMBER NOTRE
DAME." WE SHAMED THEM. IT IS NO SECRET THAT THEY'LL
BE READY. THEY ARE A PHYSICALLY BIG TEAM AND MUCH
LIKE MICHIGAN STATE IN SIZE, SPEED, AND TACTICS. IT
WILL CALL FOR A SUPERB EFFORT. ARMY WAS THE GAME

THAT ALLOWED US TO FIND OUT OUR CAPABILITIES AND
IRON OUT THE EARLIER LETHARGY. IF WE ARE TO HAVE A
GREAT SEASON - - - THIS IS ONE HELLUVA HUMP GAME
TO OVERCOME. IT WILL BE A PHYSICAL GAME WHERE EVERY
INCH AND YARD WILL BE CRUCIAL. ONLY NUMBER 4 RANKED
AUBURN HAS BEATEN MIAMI . . . BY THE SCORE OF 3 TO
0.

THEY ARE "REVENGE-MINDED," AND FIERCELY
MOTIVATED, THEY HAVE SIZE AND SKILLS - - - LOADED
WITH JUNIOR COLLEGE PEOPLE PLUS SOME "DUBIOUS
SCHOLARS" WHO JUST HAPPEN TO PLAY FOOTBALL.

IF WE PLAY WITH CHARACTER - - - POISE - - - THE
ENTHUSIASM THAT WE NOW KNOW WE ARE CAPABLE OF
HAVING - - - WE WILL WIN. IT WILL TAKE A 100%
PREPARATION EFFORT - - - PLUS AN INSPIRED GAME. SO
WHAT - - -WE'RE ALWAYS STRIVING FOR 100% EFFORT AND
WE SUDDENLY REALIZE THAT PLAYING INSPIRED IS WHAT
MAKES IT FUN. OK, MIAMI - - - COME ON, BUT DON'T
BE SHOCKED WHEN YOU WITNESS THAT WE ARE NOT ROLLING
OVER BECAUSE OF REVENGE MOTIVES, AND WE DON'T
EXPECT TO LOSE - - - BECAUSE "BABY" WE'RE NOTRE
DAME - - - AND WE'VE GOT SOME PRIDE AND THAT SAYS
IT ALL!!!

BEAT MIAMI!!!!!!!!

The Phantom

FINAL
NOTRE DAME – 38   MIAMI (FLA) – 7

NOTRE DAME VS NAVY
11/2/74, GAME #8

"THE PHANTOM SPEAKS"

SO MANY, MANY THINGS BECOME APPARENT WITH A WIN
LIKE OURS OVER MIAMI. WITH ALL OF THEIR "MOUTHING
OFF" IN THE PRESS, THEY CAME HERE WITH SIZE, SPEED,
AND SKILLS, BUT APPROACHED THE GAME WITH A PRO
EMOTION. THEY WERE NOT EXCITED, THEY DID NOT FEEL
THE THRILL OF ENTHUSIASM AND THE "GREATNESS" OF
UNITY. THIS IS PROBABLY THE ONLY THING THEY LACK,
BUT THAT IS A VERY BIG THING. THIS WAS APPARENT.

NOTRE DAME, ON THE OTHER HAND, SENSED A TOUGH-
TOUGH PHYSICAL GAME, AND GOT THEIR EMOTIONS STARTED
WITH A HARD WEEK'S WORK. WE PLAYED LIKE WE
PRACTICE, EVERYONE REALLY GIVING HIS BEST. WHEN THE
ROUTINE OF FILMS AND MEETINGS AND FIELD PRACTICE
PLUS EVEN THE ADDRESS OF THE HEAD COACH GET INTO
THE 2ND HALF OF THE SEASON, IT IS ONLY THE
EXTRAORDINARY BALL CLUB THAT CAN KEEP THE PACE. IT
IS A SUBTLE POINT, <u>IT ISN'T</u> APPARENT! IN ORDER TO
BE NOTRE DAME, IN ORDER TO BE EXTRAORDINARY, IN
ORDER TO HANDLE OURSELVES WITH DIRECTION, WE MUST
UNDERSTAND THAT "GAME DAY" IS AN EMOTIONAL SURGE.
THERE HAS TO BE A "ONE MINDEDNESS" A COMPLETE
TUNING IN TOGETHER FOR THE COMMON GOAL. THIS IS
WHAT "MAKES THINGS HAPPEN."

WAS IT EVER SO OBVIOUS AS LAST SATURDAY AGAINST
MIAMI? WE WERE READY - - - AND IT MADE IT ALL <u>FUN</u>
AND WORTHWHILE. NOW I UNDERSTAND WHAT THE GOOD LORD
MEANT WHEN HE SAID, "BE YE HOT OR COLD, BUT NOT
LUKE WARM OR I WILL SPEW YE OUT!" GREATNESS IS AN
EXTREME NOT A "MIDDLE," "BLASÉ," "LUKEWARM,"
"APATHETIC" CONDITION. IF WE CAN KEEP THE TEMPO, IF
WE UNDERSTAND THAT MOMENTUM IS MENTAL AND ANYONE
THAT DOESN'T GET CAUGHT UP IN IT HURTS US, WE CAN
GO A LONG, LONG WAY.

IN THE SECOND HALF OF THE SEASON, WE'VE POSTED
TWO REALLY GOOD GAMES. ONE AT A TIME - - - NO GAME
BEING MORE IMPORTANT THAN THE ONE WE WILL BE
PLAYING - - - WE WILL GET IT DONE.

NAVY - - - SHOOK PENN STATE. NAVY - - - ALMOST
DEFEATED PITTSBURGH. NAVY - - - IS MILITARY, STICKY
- - - PRIDEFUL. THEIR SEASON LEAVES ONLY UPSETS FOR
THEM TO GAIN STATURE. NEVER UNDERESTIMATE THE
OPPONENT. LIKE ANY OPPONENT THEY CAN RISE UP.

LET US MEANWHILE MAINTAIN THESE POSITIVE
ATTITUDES:

1. WE HAVE NO BREAKING POINT.
2. WE WILL ALWAYS APPROACH EACH GAME WITH FIERCE
   EMOTION
3. WE WILL PLAY THE WAY WE PRACTICE - - - &
   PRACTICE HARD.
4. THE END OF THE RACE IS MORE MEANINGFUL THAN
   THE BEGINNING AND WE HAVE JUST DISCOVERED
   THAT THE ENERGY NOT TO LET UP IS MAGNIFIED BY
   THE "MENTAL."

TO DO ALL THIS WOULD SET US APART. THAT IS
EXACTLY WHY NOTRE DAME IS NOTRE DAME- - - AND WHY
EACH OF YOU ARE A PART OF IT - - -. IT IS
WORTHWHILE TO CLING HARD TO THE CONCEPT THAT MAKES
US "<u>UNCOMMON</u>"!

BEAT NAVY!!!!!!!!

The Phantom

FINAL
NOTRE DAME – 14   NAVY – 6

NOTRE DAME VS PITTSBURGH
11/16/74, GAME #9

"THE PHANTOM SPEAKS"

MORE THAN EVER BEFORE IN MY LIFETIME I AM AWARE
OF JUST HOW <u>EMPTY</u> - - - ARE WORDS. WE USED WORDS
TO TELL YOU IT IS AN "EMOTIONAL GAME." WE TRIED TO
EXPLAIN THAT NO TEAM WILL ROLL OVER FOR YOU - - -
THAT THEY PLAY THEIR HIGHEST KEYED GAME AGAINST
YOU. <u>WORDS</u> ARE NOT THE ANSWER - - - <u>UNDERSTANDING
IS</u>! NO ONE MOTIVATES ANOTHER - - - MOTIVATION COMES
FROM WITHIN OURSELVES! I AM AT A LOSS TO UNDERSTAND
HOW IT IS THAT A GREAT BUNCH OF YOUNG MEN ON A
TEAM CANNOT REALIZE HOW FLEETING IS THEIR TIME TO
PLAY. WHEN IT IS OVER, IT IS OVER, AND THAT IS IT.
I AM HEARTSICK THAT OUR TEAM CANNOT ACCEPT "HUNGER"
AND "HUSTLE" AND "CONCENTRATION" AND "SELL-OUT
EFFORT" EVERY TIME WE TAKE THE FIELD. WE ARE NOT
<u>DUMB</u> PEOPLE TO BE DUPED BY PRESS CLIPPINGS AND ODDS
MAKERS - - -! STILL - - - WE WALK TO THE LINE, WE
GO 1/2 SPEED ON FAKES, WE DON'T REALLY SELL OUT.
THE "PROFESSIONALISM ATTITUDE OF A MIAMI" IS THE
MOST DISCOURAGING THING I'VE EVER SEEN FOR COLLEGE
FOOTBALL. WE LOOKED AND PLAYED VERSUS NAVY AS MIAMI
DID AGAINST US.

<u>SUSTAIN</u> — A SEVEN-LETTER WORD THAT SIGNIFIES
"READY TO PLAY." WE GOT OUT-HUSTLED AND OUT-HIT. WE
WERE DAMNED LUCKY!

NAVY IS OVER WITH - - - BUT LOOKOUT - - -
BECAUSE PITT - - - WHO IS BIG AND FAST AND
TALENTED COMES HERE TO PLAY. THEY ARE COACHED BY
WHAT I CONSIDER AN "OUTLAW" WHO USES PEOPLE TO GAIN
THINGS INSTEAD OF USING THINGS TO GAIN PEOPLE. HE
IS SETTING HIS TEAM TO KNOCK US OFF. I SEE THE
INSIDE KNOWING HOW BADLY THEY DESERVE A THRASHING.
WHAT IF WE GO AT IT WITH THE BLAH ATTITUDE AGAIN?
WHAT IF WORDS ARE NOT ENOUGH TO ENLIGHTEN YOU?

YOU HAVE JUST THREE MORE GAMES TO PLAY IN THE
1974 SEASON. WE ARE ON THE THRESHOLD OF A GREAT
SEASON - - - BUT WHO KNOWS BETTER THAN YOU OUR
INCONSISTENT EFFORT AND EXECUTION. HOW VERY, VERY

SAD - - - THAT WE CANNOT FULLY REALIZE WITH
FORESIGHT - - - THE <u>DESIRE</u> THAT HINDSIGHT <u>LEAVES</u>.
   THIS WILL BE A HUGE TASK, BEATING PITT. IF WE
HAVE THE RIGHT - - - AND THE ABILITY TO GET <u>UP</u>
- - - REALLY UP FOR A GAME; I HOPE IT WILL BE FOR
OUR LAST THREE GAMES, BECAUSE - - - WE HAVEN'T
TILL NOW. WHEN IS IT OUR TURN TO GET SKY HIGH?
WHEN DO THE GOOD GUYS GET EMOTIONALLY EXCITED?
   I LEAVE YOU THE CHALLENGE - - - FOR 3 LAST
GAMES - - - PITT — AIR FORCE — SOUTHERN CAL; BUT
IF YOU CAN'T BOTHER FOR PITT, YOU'LL HAVE GONE THE
WAY OF OTHERS. OUR ENTIRE YEAR'S WORK BOILS DOWN TO
THE FINISH OF THE YEAR.
   I HAVE NEVER LOST CONFIDENCE IN US, BUT FRANKLY
FEEL IT IS THE TEAM'S DUTY AND RIGHT TO DO
SOMETHING FOR ITSELF NOW!!!
   EACH SENIOR - - - STOOP A LITTLE AND GET
EMOTIONAL - - - WE NEED IT!!
               DO — YOU — WANT — IT?
               BEAT PITT!!!!!!!!!

The Phantom

FINAL
NOTRE DAME – 14   PITTSBURGH – 10

NOTRE DAME VS AIR FORCE
11/23/74, GAME #10

"THE PHANTOM SPEAKS"

WHEN THE CHIPS WERE DOWN, AND YOU HAD TO
PERFORM, YOU DID! A WIN, IS A WIN, IS A WIN, IS A
WIN! WE WON AND DOWN DEEP KNEW WE DID IT WITHOUT
BEING AT OUR BEST.

MISTAKES: 2 FUMBLES LOST, ONE INTERCEPTION, ONE
BLOCKED KICK. EVERY DRIVE HAD TO BE A LONG ONE.
THE LINE OF SCRIMMAGE MUST BE WON BY KNOWING
CADENCE AND OFFENSIVE HIT OUT! THIS IS THE KEY
OFFENSIVE ADVANTAGE THAT CAUSES A BUBBLE IN THE
DEFENSE. WE MUST GET AFTER IT - - - VERSUS AIR
FORCE & SOUTHERN CAL.

EACH LAST HOME GAME OF A SEASON REPRESENTS THE
LAST TIME SENIORS WILL EVER WALK THE STADIUM TURF
AS PLAYERS. IT IS A LANDMARK AND IT IS THE CLOSE
OF A HOME CAREER. THE MEMORY YOU WALK AWAY WITH
FROM THE LAST GAME AT HOME LINGERS ON FOR YEARS.
LET US PREPARE WELL AND HAVE A THUMPING GOOD SOUND
WIN.

JOHN MURPHY, IN SCOUTING AIR FORCE, IN HIS
CANDID AND INIMITABLE STYLE, SAYS THEY ARE THE BEST
LOSING TEAM HE HAS SEEN AND CANNOT IMAGINE WHY
THEIR RECORD IS NOT BETTER. HE LIKENS THEM TO NAVY.
QUICK - - - FIERCE - - - DETERMINED.

OUR CHORE & TASK IS TO IMPROVE — TO PERFORM —
TO EXECUTE WITH THE FEWEST ERRORS POSSIBLE.
HIT OUT WITH CADENCE.

1. EXPLODE INTO THE OPPONENT WITH PROPER
   TECHNIQUE AND ASSIGNMENT COMPETENCY.
2. SUSTAIN AN INTERVAL THAT IS EXTRA EFFORT FOR
   OTHERS BUT "NORMAL" FOR YOU.
3. NO TURNOVERS — SOUND DEFENSE & EXPLOSIVE
   OFFENSE, SOUND KICKING GAME . . . THESE
   THINGS WIN IN EXACTLY THE PROPORTION THEY ARE
   GIVEN.
4. GIVE YOUR BEST EFFORT - - - CALL UPON YOUR
   PERSONAL PRIDE, PLAY WITH A FULL NOTRE DAME
   HEART ON EVERY PLAY - - - AS WE TRIED TO DO

IN THE LAST 15 MIN. VERSUS PITT.

NO GAME IS EASY - - - FOR NOTRE DAME — BECAUSE WE ARE NOTRE DAME. THAT IS A KNOWN PRICE WE PAY, BUT IF WE EXPECT THIS & KNOW THIS & WORK TOWARD THIS - - - WE WILL WIN! THE SEASON IS 3 GAMES FROM ENDING. THREE CHALLENGES ON THREE DIFFERENT WEEKS — TO BE TAKEN ONE AT A TIME. THREE STEPS TO "GREATNESS."

WE CANNOT STUMBLE OR FALTER, WE CANNOT REST OR LET UP, BECAUSE IT ALL BOILS DOWN TO FINISH OFF A <u>RACE</u> THAT WE HAVE ALL RUN VERY WELL. THE FINISH LINE IS IN SIGHT AND WE ARE CALLING UPON RESERVE HEART & STRENGTH, NERVE & SINEW TO SPURT A FINAL BURST THAT WILL ALLOW US TO FINISH 1ST. IF I SAID THAT YOU HAVE A CHANCE TO REACH OUT FOR A SLICE OF HUMAN IMMORTALITY, A CHANCE TO TAKE 3 STEPS TO A PERCH OF GRIDIRON GREATNESS THAT WILL FOLLOW YOU ALL YOUR LIFE . . . AND IT WAS TO BE DONE ONE BIG STEP AT A TIME . . . CAN YOU SUCK UP YOUR GUTS, SET YOUR MIND AND HEART AND GET IT DONE?

OUR SEASON IS A SUCCESS IF IT ENDS NOW . . . IT CAN BE A UNIQUE, OUTSTANDING AND LONG REMEMBERED ONE WITH TRUE - - - TEAM EFFORT.

VERY FEW PEOPLE HAVE OUR OPPORTUNITY FOR SUCH A SHOT AT GREATNESS... AND IT RARELY COMES TO A PERSON TWICE IN ONE LIFETIME. OUR TIME IS NOW . . . OUR TEAM IS IN THE RACE AND NO OPPONENT CAN OVERCOME US IF WE REFUSE TO LET IT HAPPEN.

WHEN ALL TEAM MEN UNDERSTAND FULLY THIS OPPORTUNITY & TOTALLY DEDICATE THEMSELVES TO A FINAL GOAL — NO POWER ON EARTH CAN OPPOSE IT. MEN MAKE DESTINY MORE OFTEN THAN DESTINY MAKES THE MAN. HERE IS YOUR SHOT - - - HERE IS YOUR FIRST OF 3 STEPS —

BEAT AIR FORCE!!!

The Phantom

FINAL
NOTRE DAME – 38   AIR FORCE – 0

163

NOTRE DAME VS SOUTHERN CAL
11/30/74, GAME #11

"THE PHANTOM SPEAKS"

WE HAVE TAKEN ONE GIANT STEP IN OUR PLANNED
SERIES OF THREE - - - AND NOW FOR NUMBER TWO. NO
ONE GIVES NOTRE DAME MUCH CHANCE OF BEATING
SOUTHERN CAL. IN THE MANY YEARS - - - WE HAVE
PLAYED WE ARE FINALLY AN UNDERDOG. JUST AS WHEN WE
ARE MADE 30 POINTS A FAVORITE, THIS UNDERDOG ROLE
IS AN OPINION.

WE ARE WALKING INTO A SITUATION WHERE NO ONE
EXCEPT THOSE WHO REALLY COUNT FIGURE WE CAN DO IT.
WE - - - THE PLAYERS, THE COACHES KNOW WE CAN! A
GREAT EFFORT - - - A GREAT FEAT - - - STARTS FIRST
IN MIND. THE IDEA EXPLODES IN THE THINKING PROCESS,
IT CROWDS OUT THE MAYBES AND THE IFS. IT TAKES OUT
EVERYTHING NEGATIVE AND DWELLS ON, WE WILL DO IT!

THE MIND HARNESSES ENERGY AND STORES IT UP. THE
BODY PREPARES AND PRACTICES AND WORKS AT THE
PREPARATION. IT SLOWLY EBBS TOWARDS THE CLIMAX AND
THEN WITH FULL HEART AND FULL TEAM HARMONY - - -
EXPLODES AT THE GAME! ALL GREAT EFFORTS AND ALL
GREAT ACHIEVEMENTS ARE PRODUCTS OF READINESS. WHEN
THE IDEA OF "WIN" HITS, AND WHEN IT IS COUPLED
WITH FIERCE DETERMINATION, NO POWER CAN WITHSTAND
SUCH READINESS.

SURE, THEY ARE BIG AND FAST; SURE, IT IS THEIR
HOME FIELD; SURE, THEY ARE SMARTING FROM LAST
YEAR'S LOSS. THIS ONLY CAUSES DOUBTS IN THEIR MIND.
DOUBT IS THE ENEMY. BELIEVE IN YOURSELVES. BELIEVE
IN THE "STOUT-HEARTED" IDEA OF TEAM WALKING IN
- - - DOING THE JOB AND WALKING OUT VICTORIOUSLY.

VICTOR HUGO ONCE SAID, "NO ARMY IS AS POWERFUL
AS AN IDEA WHOSE TIME HAS COME." THEY ARE NO ARMY
AND OUR TIME HAS COME!

WHAT IS SIZE? HELL, IF SIZE WERE EVERYTHING,
ELEPHANTS WOULD RULE THE WORLD. WE ARE GOING TO
OUT-HIT, OUT-HEART, AND OUT-HUSTLE SOUTHERN CAL. WE
ARE GOING TO BE SUCH A BONDED AND CEMENTED GROUP
OF TEAM, THAT NO ONE WILL PENETRATE US. TOTAL

164

UNITY, TOTAL CONCENTRATION AND EFFORT ARE OUR
GOALS, AND WITH THESE WE WILL WIN!

ELEVEN INDIVIDUALS CAN BE BIGGER - - - FASTER
- - - AND MORE TALENTED, BUT INDIVIDUALS CANNOT
MATCH THE HARMONY OF ONE "TEAM" WITH ONE "MIND" AND
ONE "GOAL."

IN OUR FLEETING LIFETIMES ONLY RARE
OPPORTUNITIES PRESENT THEMSELVES FOR MOMENTS OF
GREAT ACHIEVEMENT. THOUGH OPPORTUNITY KNOCKS OR
WHISPERS - - - FEW ARE AWARE OF IT WHEN IT DOES.
WE HAVE THAT ADVANTAGE — WE KNOW THE OPPORTUNITY
AND THRILL AT THE CHALLENGE FOR SUCH A CHANCE. THE
WORLD'S FOOTBALL EYE IS ON US. FEW GIVE US HOPE.
THOSE WHO DO NOT CANNOT LOOK INTO OUR HEARTS NOR
KNOW THE MAGNITUDE OF OUR "TEAM DESIRE."

THESE ARE THE "ALMOST DIDS" OR PERHAPS "NEVER
CAN" — THEY NEVER DISCOVERED THE MYSTERY OF BELIEF
AND FAITH IN THEMSELVES. THEY ALLOWED DOUBT! YOU
LOSE OR GET BEAT OR GET BLOCKED OR TACKLED ONLY
BECAUSE YOU THINK IT FIRST.

YOU CAN NEVER BE BEATEN IF YOU REFUSE TO THINK
IT AND FIGHT TO NEVER LET IT HAPPEN.

WITH A FULL HEART — WITH A GREAT EMOTION — AND
A CHAMPION'S POISE - - - LET'S GO BEAT THE HELL
OUT OF SOUTHERN CAL!!!!

BEAT SOUTHERN CAL!!!!!!!

The Phantom

FINAL
NOTRE DAME – 24   SOUTHERN CAL – 55

THE ORANGE BOWL
NOTRE DAME VS ALABAMA
1/1/1975, GAME #1

"THE PHANTOM SPEAKS"

NO ONE THAT UNDERSTANDS FOOTBALL AND OUR UNIQUE
SITUATION CAN VIEW THE UPCOMING GAME WITH ALABAMA
AS ANYTHING LESS THAN A GREAT OPPORUTUNITY.

IT IS AN OPPORTUNITY TO CLOSE THE SEASON ON A
SWEETER NOTE THAN WE HAD ON THE WEST COAST. IT IS
A CHANCE AGAIN TO PLAY THE NUMBER ONE RANKED TEAM
ON NATIONAL T.V. GREAT REWARDS GO HAND-IN-HAND WITH
GREAT CHALLENGES.

NO ONE GIVES YOU A CHANCE. THE STAFF AT N.D.
- - - TEAM MEMBERS AND THE PHANTOM SEE THINGS
UNLIKE THE VIEWING PUBLIC. WE HAVE A GREAT CHANCE!
WE HAVE MORE THAN A GREAT CHANCE TO BEAT ALABAMA.

THE SEVERE LOSS TO SOUTHERN CAL WAS NOT OUR
"NORMAL" GAME. WE KNOW THIS - - - BUT NO ONE ELSE
DOES. WE ARE CAPABLE OF BEATING ANY COLLEGE
FOOTBALL TEAM ON ANY GIVEN DAY.

PEOPLE ON THE OUTSIDE LOOKING IN, THINK SOUTHERN
CAL OVERPOWERED US. THEY REALLY DON'T UNDERSTAND
THE MOMENTUM SWITCH AND THE "STUNNED" REACTION.
THEY THINK WE QUIT AND WERE THAT MUCH INFERIOR. WE
DIDN'T RELY ON THEIR OBSERVATIONS OR GUIDANCE OR
UNDERSTANDING BEFORE, AND MORE THAN EVER, SHOULD
NOT NOW. ONE THING WE'VE NEVER DONE IS QUIT, AND
GOD ONLY KNOWS WE'RE NOT INFERIOR TO ANYONE!

ALABAMA HAS GREAT SPEED! WE HAVE A LITTLE MORE
SIZE. THEY HAVE A REVENGE MOTIVE. WE HAVE ONE ALSO.
THERE IS NO OTHER WAY TO MEET THIS CHALLENGE THAN
WITH A GREAT "BOUNCE BACK" EFFORT.

ALL THE SENIORS, JUNIORS, SOPHOMORES, AND FROSH
- - - UNITED WITH GREAT HARMONY - - - AND
DEDICATION TO PLAY AN ERRORLESS GAME WITH A FULL
HEART.

"PRIDE" IS OUR KEY NOW! WE ARE NOT A "LAME
DUCK," JUST TO AFFORD AN OPPONENT TO ALABAMA - - -
BUT A FOOTBALL TEAM OF MERIT THAT PLAYS TO WIN

WHENEVER WE WALK ON THE FILLED. IN THIS CASE — IT
IS THE LAST WALK FOR THE 1974 TEAM.
MAKE A VOW - - - DO YOUR PART - - -
BEAT 'BAMA!!!!!!!!!!

The Phantom

ORANGE BOWL
FINAL
NOTRE DAME – 13   ALABAMA – 11

The Phantom's Psychology
of Winning

The Psychology of winning is not easily laid out in squared-off paragraphs that flow in a chronological order much as a recipe for brewing stew. After having spent a lifetime of attempting to win at some goals in life, watching thousands of young, hopeful athletes pursue this same quest on athletic fields . . . wage their personal life campaigns of triumph and disaster; I am struck by the complexity, yet simplicity, of winning!

Definition

Perhaps before attempting to sort through how I perceive someone attempting to prepare to win, a definition of what winning and being a winner is as opposed to losing and being a loser is . . . would be helpful. Most of the world, due to the pace of life we live, speaks in clichés or phrases that pigeon-hole people or brand them with a title that bears no resemblance to the truth. We do not lose all the way to winning or visa versa.

One who winds up on the short end of the score is not always a loser. Conversely, he who wins over all and amasses all the trophies and all the ribbons with massive scores . . . is not always the winner. It is a flawed judgment of the world at large that judges with superficial and shallow criteria.

In that vein, every time a new champion is crowned it is as though all that preceded the championship was the path of the *loser*. Now that you've won over all, should the world call you winner? Nothing could be more absurd!

The definition of winning implies a dream, a goal, a stair-

168

steps of milestones and accomplishments. It further implies dif-
ficulty to attain, worth, quality, not common . . . but rare achievement. Perhaps that is the first point in understanding the psychology of winning. Define the dream, the goal, the target.
Examine it. Is it worthwhile attaining or empty? Does it call
upon talent, sacrifice, work, dedication, loyalty, courage, planning, intellect? You can bet that if these qualities are necessary to
achieve the goal that it will not come easily nor be a common
achievement.

The definition of winning, then, that is most accurate and
most appealing to my mind is one that stipulates a high-quality
goal that presents a worthwhile challenge to the intellect of the
seeker with a reasonable and proportionate reward. Once having the goal or target in focus the contestant, before he enters the
arena, must know that *not to enter is to lose for certain*. To enter,
not with foolhardy devil may care whim, but with stockpiled
preparation is to be a winner regardless of outcome.

Winning then is simply the whole-hearted, fully dedicated,
well-placed and prepared for *ATTEMPT TO ACHIEVE A GOAL
OR SERIES OF GOALS FOR A VALUED QUALITY REASON.*

The Ingredients

When the target or goal is in focus, when the enthusiasm ripens
within the breast of the contestant and the attempt has been
determined, there are some basic pieces of armor that enhance
the odds toward success.

Knowledge

The greatest armor to possess is to know as thoroughly as possible what it is you are facing as an obstacle or barrier. Study it.
Understand it. Analyze its strength. Know its weakness and
practice against those very things. Knowing the opponent is
paramount. Otherwise we fight ghosts.

Epilogue: *The Phantom's Psychology of Winning*

Discipline

The strongest discipline individuals have are those responses that belong to them naturally, these are those habitual responses, the grooved, predictable ones. If new skills are needed, then they must be practiced over and over with an almost fanatical zest until they are not foreign but habitual.

There is a Spanish Proverb that states simply: "Habits begin as cobwebs in our minds. . . . But within two weeks they are as steel cables." Both good and bad habits can be built or broken with the discipline of proper practice. This kind of preparatory dedication is brought about by yet another ingredient.

Loyalty

The quality of loyalty is far reaching. It understands the question, "Why am I or you or anyone in this contest, this battle?" It answers that "I believe in our goal, and I understand that attaining it will extract a price . . . not only do I understand, I agree to it." The loyalty of a team member, a family member, a sole contestant is the promise to expend their greatest effort whether things go *well* or poorly. It is obviously no great feat to give loyalty as things go well. The test of loyalty is greatest when things go poorly.

Courage

To be a winner one often travels uncharted paths. There are some scary and shaky obstacles among the unfamiliar attempts to be made and it calls for a degree of risk and gamble. Most certainly . . . courage is not the absence of fear. It is having fear, and overcoming it to perform the task at hand. All great competitors, champions, winners, be they on athletic fields, or Wall Street . . . know fear and overcome it.

"The greatest hazard to life is to risk nothing. The person who risks nothing, does nothing, has nothing, is nothing!"

Perhaps unwittingly, by using that anonymous quote I have defined a "loser."

Every great thing attained calls for a payment whether it be the extracting of effort or personal sacrifice. Kahlil Gibran, the famous writer from Lebanon, wrote this classic line in the same context.

"Happiness can only be held in the hollow carved by pain."

The truth of the matter become obvious. If the attainment of a goal is worthwhile, it will extract a price. It is usually the hard work – effort – sacrifice – time and dedication that sweetens the prize. Gibran hit upon the heart of the matter with great insight.

Effort

Effort, dogged effort . . . to try . . . to try again . . . with the same or greater intensity is the mark of greatness in an athlete. So long as one tries intelligently with a solid well-planned effort there is no foe or barrier that can withstand the repeated blows of honest effort. Effort is tied to enthusiasm. Volumes have been written about enthusiasm. With it one is said to be able to move mountains. Without it – "fall upon your knees to pray for it." It is the lubricant of life. If one loves what he is about, enthusiasm flows naturally. Peggy Lee when asked to define success once said, "Success is the reward you get for loving your job!"

As a former football coach who has entered teams into contests that had national impact, I can honestly say that no thrill exceeds that of watching 80 or so young men alive with the notion of victory. They sense what they are about and perhaps for one of the rare times in their lives they are attuned to one common thought, driven by the rarified air of "enthusiastic effort." When two such teams meet, quite sure they will not be denied, no one really can lose. There never can be a total loss whenever and enthusiasm joins preparation and planning. The spin-off or by-products of such great contests have never contained anything but beneficial experiences.

171

Epilogue: *The Phantom's Psychology of Winning*

Score

Sometimes the scoreboard says you lost. Sometimes the clock runs out. If my teams saw themselves as losers because their great effort was at that moment unrewarded. . . . I failed as a coach. They, I am proud to say, did not!

Resilience

This last thought brings me to one more ingredient that the psychology of a winner must possess. People who win at things in life are never defeated mentally for very long. They have a resiliency, a "bounce," if you will, that allows them to take an 8 or 9 count, get up off the canvas and try again. Not only do I admire this great trait, I marvel at it. Examining my own life, I possessed it and I am grateful to have owned such a quality.

After the playing-field careers of people are long forgotten, their lives collide with all the traumas and tragedies of life. The sorrow that we all come to know through ourselves and our loved ones are too numerous to list. How one copes with these "slings and arrows" of life, how one bounces back from the gut=wrenching adversity we are handed, is everything!

People who don't back away from the fights of life but take them on . . . are a winning breed. They are not just men but all ages and kinds of people. The phrase I've heard and appreciated says "Tough but not toughs." That's what the winning breed, the psychology of living really is. These kinds of people do not seek "cop outs" or "escapes." They are not super-human but they believe in themselves. They know that life and the quality of life must be earned. They are aware that there will be peaks and valleys, some knockdowns and some injustices. None of those things will dampen their absolute belief in their eventual victorious outcome. Within that paragraph written, though not written beautifully, is the beauty of life.

The teams I've coached have taught it to me, and I hope in turn that I passed it on to a few others. It is called an irrepressible or indominatable spirit. It never quits or says "uncle." It never breaks. It has no breaking point.

"Will not compute" is too easy a phrase, but in truth the Champion, the winner's mind, cannot accept ultimate defeat ever! It doesn't register.

Observation

When we witness such beauty within a competitive field, it is an inspiring sight to behold. It is the 15 to 1 thoroughbred that broke badly at the gate and trails by a furlong but unfolds its birthright and breeding through the final stretch and crosses the wire in full effort regardless of finishing first or last. It was programmed to run its best. It cannot do otherwise.

It is a tired, whipped, and obviously beaten fighter that reaches down deep into the crevices where human pride and dignity dwell. He musters a reserve on raw nerve. Rudyard Kipling alludes to it within this line from "If."

> If you can force your heart and nerve and sinew
> To serve your turn long after they are gone
> And so hold on when there is nothing in you
> Except the Will which says to them: "Hold on"

Kipling had an insight into the winners breed. Within that same poem he admonished every person who went broke in the stock market crash of 1929. Whereas some took elevators to high floors and soared out of windows to the pavement because of paper fortunes lost, Kipling wrote:

> Or watch the things you gave your life to, broken,
> And stoop to build 'em up with worn-out tools.

Other men and women with the fortitude and the formula to overcome life and *not be overcome* rolled up their sleeves and began.

Their victories are legion and represent the corporate success of young America.

There is yet another example that speaks of the audacity to dare, the strength to go on. The late and great Vincent Lombardi knew that when you were not physically or otherwise prepared, you were not going to measure up to what winning demands. Though he meant it in a physical sense, it can be taken many ways. He said simply *"Fatigue makes cowards of us all!"* When you are spent, tired, drawn, bored, how will you instinctively react? The *winner* is he or she or they who run the full race, with a full heart. It was ever so and probably will always be so.

Summary

In a summary attempt to profile a specific category of a "winner or winning," the end result must be focused before effort is ever harnessed. If you know not where you are headed, it matters little which direction you take or what you do.

If what you seek to attain is CLEARLY DEFINED, if it is vividly visible, if it is constantly rehearsed in terms of success, the reality of attainment is much closer.

Once you select your goal, there must be checkpoints, alternative plans and lesser goals that lead towards the ultimate one. These need to be plotted and planned.

The unadulterated, tenacious, skilled, refined *attempt* to achieve a goal while mustering the human qualities of knowledge, discipline, loyalty, courage, effort, resilience, and observation to know where one is along the way . . . is winning!

Quite certainly there are other ingredients and I'm sure there is a correct time to add one or the other. There are elements of luck and management that an individual cannot even begin to calibrate. I do know this, however, that winning is a very human trait. It is not the property of a machine. It starts as an idea, a concept, a dream, and only humans have those. It can start with one person, a group, a company, a state, or a nation. If the idea is fed and focused, if it is within the realm of possibility, if it can ignite the loyalty of people who work to make the dream come true; it is near to happening.

Every time we discover a new cure, a better pain killer, a more successful way to educate, every time our research provides greater and more *nutritious* produce to feed our nation and other nations, we are making small but significant wins.

As a nation we may be disliked because of our arrogance, our success, but the very mouths that are critical of our apparent lack of humility are also in awe of our ability to search out new and better ways. Our energy and creativity, our competitive spirit to achieve and succeed are much envied. These very qualities are the ones that have elevated our standard of living to the highest in the world.

The true winner as a person or as a nation has a deep-seated humility not evident always to the outsider. It says "Yes, I'm good, I believe in me but I paid the price. I paid my dues. My rewards are the result of my going *through*, what it takes to win."

If that is vanity. . . . then perhaps it is yet another ingredient in the makeup of winning. It need not be paraded, advertised, or aggrandized. The truly good things in life, the world discovers of itself. Japan studied our systems for years before deciding to win for themselves.

The Human Equation

The ultimate game and the ultimate victory is a long way from the athletic fields or the Superbowl or even Wall Street. It is somewhere hidden in the heart of each man and each woman awaiting his or her own personal discovery. It is tied to a set of values within life and about life. It has to do with talent and energy and personal motivations. It has to do with the quality of effort one puts forth. Within each person is an unknown quantity and quality of physical, spiritual and mental capability.

Along the way, you sense that life is composed of many battles and that all losses and all victories are very temporary. The only time a lasting victory is to be gained in life is when a person harnesses and refines whatever God-given ability he has been given . . . and uses that talent to forward the human condition. It becomes important now, when examined in that light, that the self strives for quality in all things encompassing the family of man. What higher aspiration can there be?

I have witnessed the lives of individuals that lacked great talent. Their effort, their preparations, their unselfishness, was so apparent that it generated a great and true enthusiasm. Maybe what I've described is yet again – a kind of talent. Such enthusiasm overcame the lack of talent. It caused success, it overcame obstacles, it formed tradition and habit and fostered greater expectancy. Once having tasted victory the horizon of achievement became boundless. The formula is re-enacted every day by people who desire to succeed. They accept and refine and groom themselves. They enter the arena of life and compete with a full heart in all that they do. Is that familiar? Not lukewarm effort, mind you, but blazing hot. Winners give it everything, their best effort, with exactly what it is they've got to give.

Lastly, it is also an apparent truth in life that no one does "it" all by themselves. Truly, "no man is an island." To believe in yourself is an important thing. To like yourself is just as important. Beyond all of this is a belief in a Divine Power.

I cannot believe anyone is a winner in the true sense unless they also believe in that Divine Power and give due credit for the talents they have received in their lifetime.

It is through this Power that the world has hope . . . and the tools to want to win against disease, crime, starvation, and the other ills that plague the world.

If you believe in yourself, and in a Divine Power . . . you are a winner!

"When you lose, it isn't over. When you quit, it is over!"